The
Drummond
Brothers
A Scottish Duo

by
J.E. Chacksfield
FBIS, MRAeS, AFAIAA, C.Eng.

THE OAKWOOD PRESS

© Oakwood Press & J.E. Chacksfield 2005

British Library Cataloguing in Publication Data
A Record for this book is available from the British Library
ISBN 0 85361 632 9

Typeset by Oakwood Graphics.
Repro by Ford Graphics, Ringwood, Hants.
Printed by Cambrian Printers, Aberystwyth, Dyfed.

'T9' No. 119, the Royal engine, rests at Eastleigh in June 1935. *John Scott-Morgan Collection*

Title page: Station Square and the station frontage at Inverness as depicted in a contemporary commercial postcard. *Lens of Sutton*

Front cover: Caledonian Railway Single No. 123 'Racing between Carlisle and Edinburgh in 1888'. *John Alsop Collection*
Rear cover, top: An example of one of Peter Drummond's 'Castle' class, No. 140 *Taymouth Castle*. *Railway Magazine*
Rear cover, bottom: Dugald Drummond's 'Bug' serviced his personal transport requirements during his time on the London & South Western Railway. *John Alsop Collection*

Published by The Oakwood Press (Usk), P.O. Box 13, Usk, Mon., NP15 1YS.
E-mail: sales@oakwoodpress.co.uk
Website: www.oakwood-press.co.uk

Contents

Foreword

The careers of the Drummond brothers spanned a period of great innovation in the development of the design and management of the steam locomotive. The period began with the locomotives that were appropriate for the earliest days of the railway system, and their careers concluded at a time when locomotives were being developed that were to be the mainstays of the United Kingdom's passenger and freight transport system during the first half of the 20th century.

The contribution of the brothers to this very important period of change was led by the elder brother, Dugald, who during his early years in the railway industry, developed a sound basic understanding of the principles of steam locomotive design and management. He also possessed good organizational ability, which was to be demonstrated by the improvements he planned and implemented at the main workshops that came under his responsibility.

It is safe to assume that these attributes were amply demonstrated to the younger brother, Peter, during the 20 year period that they worked together, and that this provided Peter with a sound basis for his contribution once he assumed responsibility as a Locomotive Superintendent in his own right.

Dugald Drummond had a very gruff and uncompromising approach, but he is also remembered as someone who would be mindful of the personal circumstances of his staff, and for the interest he took in developing training and education. He both demonstrated and expected high standards in the workplace.

Whilst some of Dugald's innovative design features did not always benefit the maintenance and overall performance of his locomotives, his basic design principles of robustness and standardisation of components led to some of his locomotives remaining in service until the second half of the 20th century. The years immediately following his death were to provide the opportunity for the further development of some of his locomotives, and the reappraisal of some of the designs and innovations that were not successful.

His successor at Eastleigh, Robert Urie, who had been closely associated with Dugald as his Works Manager at St Rollox, Nine Elms and Eastleigh, was to design and build locomotives that incorporated the basic design principles of robustness and standardisation of components. The Urie locomotives, however, were different in that they were designed for ease of maintenance, and would prove to be reliable and versatile locomotives that were to remain in active service until the final days of steam locomotive operation on British Railways.

The Drummond Brothers is a compelling account of two people who, in their own individual ways, successfully progressed the design, construction and management of steam locomotives so that they were able to meet the ever-increasing traffic demands being placed upon their owning railway companies. The book provides an illuminating insight into the lives of the brothers, and John Chacksfield is to be congratulated on achieving this most interesting account of the contribution the two brothers made to the development of the locomotive and carriage stock of their time.

Robert Urie
(Grandson)
January 2005

4

Introduction

For 42 years the Drummond brothers were engaged in designing locomotives for a range of Scottish- and English-based railways, Dugald from 1875 to 1912 and Peter from 1896 to 1918. In total they bequeathed over 1,100 locomotives to the British railway scene, some of them classics and many at the forefront of locomotive technology appropriate to the time.

Whilst Dugald eventually based himself in England, Peter preferred to remain in his native Scotland for the majority of his career, which was somewhat eclipsed by that of his older brother's forthright approach to design matters. He learnt a lot from studying Dugald's designs and, in some cases, adapted them for his own use. To this end he was often aided by Dugald supplying sets of drawings of his latest designs to assist in his deliberations. Be that as it may, Peter's temperament did not quite match that of Dugald. His life was less fraught with episodes of undiplomatic handling of events and he was not so renowned for some harsh treatment of offenders who questioned or, sometimes, ignored his authority. Those who dared to do either with Dugald rarely survived in office long before their transfer or summary dismissal appeared. The type of person who seemed to brush off all invective aimed in their direction was the one who displayed cool, but polite, reasoning in a calm and ordered manner - they were the ones who survived the onslaught. Such persons were rare, but existed, as we shall see.

During the research for this biography, it has become apparent that, despite his reputation for blunt outspokenness, Dugald had a deeply human and understanding side to his nature, having had several personal tragedies in his own life. A past master at 'carpeting' those deserving disciplinary treatment, he could also show leniency where it was needed. His bark was most definitely worse than his bite in many cases, but that was the nature of the man.

Peter Drummond, on the other hand, has been overshadowed by his elder brother and thought of as a mediocre Chief Mechanical Engineer (CME). Despite this, it would be unfair to leave him out of the story, for his efforts in Scotland were certainly notable and his life in that land merits a comprehensive record.

The toughness of Drummond locomotives was legendary - it was said that you could drop one off a viaduct only to find a bent cab side-sheet on recovery - and many examples of Dugald's, although designed in Victorian days, lived on into Nationalisation, as if to epitomise their designer's outright feelings.

It took a tough engineman to cross swords with a Drummond, but when he had the guts to stand up to Dugald's tirade, he was rewarded with understanding and support should he be proved correct, or if there were extraneous circumstances affecting his personal performance. Both the brothers handled men competently and firmly, sometimes too firmly, in the works environment and were excellent organizers. Dugald was the greater personality by far and his reputation was firmly established by the time Peter rose to high office and his efforts tended to overshadow those of his younger brother. Nevertheless, their combined stories are an important episode in the annals of railway history and, in this book, are drawn together to provide a picture of their respective lives and achievements. It is hoped that the chronicle of Peter's career will put him in the position rightly due to him as an experienced CME of two of the pre-Grouping Scottish railways.

The fascinating thing about this biography, for Dugald at least, was that the deeper one dug for background and family information the more one found of great personal tragedies in his life. Tragedies which would have floored many others, yet here was a resilient character who overcame them and continued to forge a great career. The character shines through these events in the deep understanding of those under his control who suffered similarly: a human person.

Researching his biography has proved a lengthy task and the author wishes to thank the Mitchell Library in Glasgow and the Libraries in Ardrossan, Falkirk and Inverness for steady support. Also the Australian adventure of Dugald was assisted by the prompt and generous supply of such information as exists with the successor company to that with which he was involved during his brief interlude Down Under. His enticement from the safe confines of the Caledonian Railway Works at St Rollox and the resulting adventure in the suburbs of Sydney is, at last, chronicled to a greater degree of certainty.

This book has been a difficult one to lay out, for the brothers worked closely together, on the same railways, for 20 years before going their own ways. The division comes in 1890 with Dugald's departure for Australia. After this time, I have treated their careers as two separate stories, Dugald coming first, followed by a step back in time to pick up the more limited, but still worthy of note, career of Peter.

I would like to thank Robert Urie for his Foreward and his thorough reading of my draft text.

Finally, I must thank those who provided the illustrations for this book, in particular Jim Jarvis for supplying a good number of his own and the late Ron Jarvis' photos. The *Railway Magazine* also kindly consented that some of their magazines could be plundered for some historic works' and other pictures covering the Highland Railway (HR) episodes of both Dugald and Peter. Lastly, the archives held by John Alsop, Roger Carpenter and John Scott-Morgan were well used, bringing some classic pictures into the book.

A rare combination this. Dugald Drummond class '264' 0-4-0ST hauls Peter Drummond 'Castle' No. 14686 *Urquhart Castle* fresh from the paint shop. Date unknown, but thought to be *c.*1930.   *Jarvis Collection/J. Rutherford*

Chapter One

Early Days

The name Drummond has long been that of one of the old established clans of Scotland. The legend is that the Drummonds are descended from one Yorik de Marot, the Royal Admiral to Hungary and grandson of King Andrew of Hungary. Yorik journeyed to the shores of Scotland in the depths of winter to deliver Margaret, future queen of Scotland, into the hands of Malcolm Canmore in the early 11th century. She was the grand-daughter of Edmond Ironside, himself the son of Edgar, King of Wessex from 959-75. This marriage began the Anglicisation of Scotland, a long process which only came to a conclusion in 1603.

Yorik's descendant, Malcolm Begg, or 'Little Malcolm', became the Thane of Lennox in the 13th century and his son, Sir Malcolm (de Drymen), took the name Drummond. For many centuries the Drummonds were loyal to Scotland and her Kings, serving the houses of Bruce and Stuart for over 500 years. Drummond ladies were noted for their beauty, with two becoming Queens of Scotland. The family was also well-known for their temper. 'From the ire of the Drummonds, Good Lord, deliver us' was a frequent prayer offered up in the 17th century.

The long years of faithful service resulted in James, in 1605, after he had been crowned King of England and Scotland, elevating the chief of the Drummond clan to the Earl of Perth. To the end the Drummonds supported the Stuarts and were involved in the rising of 1746, following Bonnie Prince Charlie to Culloden. The defeat by the English there scattered the clan leaders and it was not until 1784 that their lands, and in 1830 their titles, were restored to them.

Nearly 800 years of growth had ensured the spread of the Drummond name throughout Scotland. Family members were to be found in all levels of society.

In north Ayrshire there is a group of small towns on or near the coast which faces south-westwards over the Firth of Clyde - Ardrossan, Saltcoats, Stevenston, Kilwinning and Irvine. Some 10 miles away across the water lies the mountainous island of Arran to which one may travel by ferry from the small port of Ardrossan. Steamer services ran, and still run, to the Isle of Man and there was also a regular service to Liverpool before the railways provided speedier transport between Scotland and England.

The small harbour used by the ferries and steamers was, for many years, served by a connection off the branch line to Largs, the junction being just outside of Ardrossan station. This Largs branch and its sub-branch was part of what became the Glasgow and South Western Railway (G&SWR) and fed the small towns along the Firth of Clyde with thousands of Glaswegians taking holiday breaks or days out 'doon the watter'.

Ardrossan was one of the first ports in Scotland to be connected to a major city by rail, in this instance Glasgow. There had been plans to construct the Ardrossan Canal between the two places, but the construction of this only reached Johnstone, about one-third of the distance to be covered, when a proposal for the Ardrossan Railway was mooted in 1819 by the 12th Earl of

Eglinton who owned much of the land across which it was to pass. The railway was proposed to run from Ardrossan and connect with the canal at Johnstone. Little happened until 1826 when the proposal was put before Parliament and received Royal Assent on 12th June, 1827. There were a couple of waggonways, one at Ardrossan itself and the other at nearby Kilwinning which were absorbed into the Ardrossan Railway. In 1829 construction began of the 5½ mile stretch between Ardrossan and Kilwinning, the initial line being laid as a 4 ft 6 in. gauge waggonway. By 1840 ten locomotives were at work on a line now 22 miles long. In that year the Glasgow, Paisley, Kilmarnock & Ayr Railway was opened. This motivated the Ardrossan Railway to re-build to the standard gauge to enable connection at Kilwinning to this main line. With Ardrossan's steamer connections to Liverpool and the Isle of Man the ability to run trains through to Glasgow ensured the prosperity of the Ardrossan Railway.

On 30th November, 1838 a George Drummond married the woman in his life, Christina Thompson, at the Ardrossan Parish Church in accordance with the rites and customs of the Church of Scotland, officiated by the Revd Boyce, and it was in that small but busy port that the newly-weds set up home and settled back to await developments. It was not long in coming, for it was on 2nd January, 1840 that Dugald, their first child, entered the World, to be christened by the Revd Boyce at the Church where his parents wed, on 26th January that year. The year 1840 was notable for the introduction of the Penny Post, which revolutionised communication throughout the British Isles, now that the rapidly expanding railways were appearing as a means of speedy transport compared to the stagecoaches or postal riders. It was also the year in which the Peninsular & Oriental Steamship Company started the first steamer service to India, via the Cape, for the Suez Canal was still a dream in de Lesseps' head. The increase in trade that this and other world-wide connections caused resulted in the yearly total of exports of the growing industries of the British Isles rising to £197 million (£23.6 billion today) in a single decade. Imports were also growing, with £100 million (£12 billion) worth of materials and goods landed for distribution over the fledgling railway system.

Dugald's father was shortly to be employed by the Ardrossan Railway on the civil engineering side, involving the permanent way. In those days it was quite common for a son, or sons, to follow in his father's footsteps. For Dugald this was to be a natural progression, as from an early age he expressed an interest in entering the railway profession.

This was the time in the British Isles when railway expansion was starting the rise to its zenith. The industrial confines of nearby Glasgow were spreading ever outwards, demanding more transport infrastructure, with the railways in that area prospering and expanding as they served the factories, shipyards and collieries together with the associated workforce. Prospects were good and a job on the railways that flourished would mean steady, continuous, employment.

However, the Drummond family continued to grow, for in 1842 a sister, Jane, arrived as company for two-year-old Dugald who was, by then, becoming quite mobile and adventurous.

By the middle of the 1840s the Drummonds had moved to Polmont near Grangemouth, Dugald's father having transferred his services to the newly-opened Edinburgh and Glasgow Railway (EGR). Polmont is situated almost half-way between Glasgow and Edinburgh and lies a few miles south of the innermost reaches of the Firth of Forth, and had grown from a group of settlements, Old Polmont, Bennetstown and Brightons. When the EGR arrived the community blossomed and the local industry was boosted by the service the railway provided. The wealth generated by all this industrial success brought to Polmont some fine houses and estates amongst which was Millfield, built by John Millar, who was to become the Secretary of the North British Railway (NBR). This house, like so many others, has been swept away to make room for post-war housing and commercial developments. Polmont has changed dramatically from the brief years that the Drummonds lived there. It was here, in 1850, that a brother for Dugald and Jane, Peter, was born. Peter was to be drawn into the engineering side of the railways and follow his elder brother's vocation, as will be recounted later. The railway system throughout the British Isles passed the 5,000 mile mark in that year, on its way to an eventual total of over 30,000 miles by the end of the 19th century.

Dugald's schooling, which commenced seriously in Polmont, probably at Polmont Parish School, which seems to have enjoyed a good reputation, indicated a preference and ability for any subject liable to be of use for engineering as a career. He began to firm up his desire to take up that profession, clearly encouraged by his father.

A few years after Peter was born, the Drummonds moved yet again, this time to Maryhill in the Northern suburbs of Glasgow. The exact date is not known apart from it being before 1855, as in that year Peter began his education at Maryhill Public School. This move was brought about by George Drummond obtaining a senior position of inspector of permanent way on the Caledonian and Dumbartonshire Junction Railway (C&DJR). This new line, opened in 1850, ran from Balloch at the southern extremity of Loch Lomond to Bowling on the eastern side of the River Clyde just outside Glasgow. This new home in Maryhill was fortuitous, for there were many engineering works to hand. George Drummond cast around for suitable companies in the locality and, as schooling finished, an apprenticeship with Messrs Forrest and Barr at their Canal Street Engineering Works, Glasgow was arranged for Dugald. Amongst the general engineering work carried out here was a certain amount of locomotive construction for the many railways spreading throughout the UK at that time. After a hard day's work in that plant, a 10-hour day being not uncommon then, Dugald could be found trudging some distance to the nearest Technical College where he had enrolled to embark on a course of Mechanical Drawing, the better to learn something of the art of design.

This way of collecting his technical education made him, in later years, resolve to do something about the lack of such opportunities for apprentices who wished to go further than the shop floor environment for, in those days, an apprenticeship tended to be strongly biased towards the shop floor and the tasks of production. This decision of Dugald's will be described fully in Chapter Seven. He obviously had, at this stage, an ambition to advance his career beyond the purely skilled manual work for which he was being trained.

Five years were spent in the noisy clatter of the shop floor of Forrest & Barr and, after completing his apprenticeship and wishing to broaden his knowledge, he left that concern and joined his father for a short while on the C&DJR , which was eventually to be absorbed into the Caledonian Railway. After a short time of engagement in matters revolving around track and signalling maintenance he moved on again. The next job was across the border in Birkenhead, with Messrs Peto, Brassey and Betts. Amongst its varied engineering output this company built locomotives for the home and export markets and was to provide good experience in the practicalities of production methods, so that should he get to the design stage, he would be the better able to devise components which would present easy tasks to those manufacturing them. He started in the boiler shop amidst the noisy clangour of drilling and riveting boiler plates and firebox shells. Peto, Brassey and Betts were ultimately responsible for the construction of over one-sixth of the entire railway network in the UK. It was, certainly, an influential concern by which to be employed.

Dugald soon made his presence felt not only by his forthright comments and tall stature but by his natural aptitude for organizing other colleagues' tasks. This did not go unnoticed by the foremen under whom he worked and promotion to chargehand followed. No matter what size of gang he had charge over, his control of them and their tasks showed a born leader at work. At this level he was insulated from those in higher management and his outspoken comments were absorbed by the middle management, most of whom had come up from the shop floor and were well versed in such things.

Two years were profitably spent at Birkenhead as he gradually rose through the lower ranks of fitters, chargehands and foremen towards the esteemed heights of works management. Then in 1863, having gained a considerable amount of expertise in the skills of handling gangs of workmen, he returned to his native Scotland and the Cowlairs works of the Edinburgh & Glasgow Railway. Whilst employed at Birkenhead it was in nearby Liverpool that Dugald became acquainted with Jane Young and began courting her. Jane had been born in Southerness, near Dumfries, in 1841, the daughter of a mariner. The friendship blossomed and Jane eventually consented to marry him, once he had a steady job back on the railways, for engineering industry was prone to ups and downs not normally associated with the railways.

At Cowlairs the Locomotive Superintendent was none other than Samuel Johnson, later to hold the same position at Derby on the Midland Railway. Johnson had as his Works Manager a fellow Englishman, William Stroudley.

Stroudley's correct, kindly, disposition and dignified manners contrasted with Dugald's blunt, Lowland Scottish upbringing nourished by experiences on the shop floor. Also a tall man, he could look Dugald straight in the eye. Both soon realised each other's potential after a few weeks working together in close proximity (Dugald had been appointed one of Stroudley's several assistants). As so often happens in cases like this, they got on. Drummond could certainly manage men, and Stroudley quickly latched on to this to ensure that the production he was charged with appeared on time, on cost and, more importantly, of adequate quality. Likewise, Dugald respected his superior's engineering abilities and made sure he learnt all he could by watching, listening to, and acting upon the sound decision-making he encountered.

Compared to Stroudley, Samuel Johnson, on the other hand, was rather autocratic and tended to keep his Works Manager at arm's length. Perhaps he saw a potential threat to his own position from a clearly competent manager, for more often than not the Locomotive Superintendent was selected from that position. This divide-and-rule philosophy pressed upon the two top men, with each man's followers keeping closely to their mentor's policies, was a recipe for polarisation which was bound to end in strife. It happened this way. Following application for the post of Locomotive Superintendent of the Highland Railway, Stroudley was chosen out of no fewer than 31 aspiring candidates, and accepted it. The previous incumbent on the HR, William Barclay, had resigned and temporarily departed from the railway scene.

Upon Johnson's announcement of the impending move, the workmen began to collect together for a parting present to a clearly popular Works Manager. Dugald entered into this with some considerable vigour and, deciding that this parting gift should be subscribed to by all at the works, went in to see if Johnson cared to contribute from the inner confines of his office. The story goes that Johnson was not feeling in a generous mood that day, probably smarting at the forthcoming loss of a valuable officer, refused to give anything, saying: 'I'm damned if I will'. The reply from Dugald was less than complimentary, implying that Johnson was already of that ilk, following which he marched briskly out, slamming the door behind him. Johnson recovered from this withering Drummond blast and called his clerk in to order Dugald's immediate dismissal. However, he found himself thwarted in that, for a resignation had already been lodged on the way out. Dugald's respect for Stroudley was clearly evident in this extreme outburst to Johnson, as was his own realisation that such talk was just not acceptable.

Also, the previous month Dugald had returned to Liverpool and on the 2nd June, 1865 married Jane at St Mary's church in Edge Hill. The best man was, suitably, Jane's brother David and the bridesmaid Dugald's sister, Jane. However, his episode with Johnson rather upset matters and almost immediately after settling in Scotland they had to uproot and go further North for Stroudley, being a fair-minded and honourable man, did not wish to see a newly-wed young couple put into hard times, no matter how temporary. So, in July 1865, Stroudley found himself accompanied by Dugald to Inverness, where he placed him as foreman-erector in the Lochgorm works there. It is immediately apparent that Stroudley had been impressed by the vigour and organizational skill in Drummond and felt that he could make good use of these talents in Inverness. Dugald and Jane set up home in one of a row of houses in Tomnahurich Street owned by Alexander Matheson, MP. This street lay across the River Ness from the site of the station and works. It would have been a long enough walk to work in the depths of winter at the early starting hour of probably 6.00 am. For neighbours they had many railway staff, from engine crews to fitters and turners from the works.

Lochgorm works sat just outside the station throat at Inverness. The combined station and works site had, in years past, been reclaimed from a small expanse of water known as Loch Gorm. The works themselves were bounded by a triangle of lines consisting of the two approaches to the station, one from Wick, the other from Aberdeen and Perth, and the connecting track of the through loop line. Space was at a premium and the works were always limited in their size, and hence output, because of this. The carriage and wagon shops were located across the loop line on a plot of land known as Needlefield.

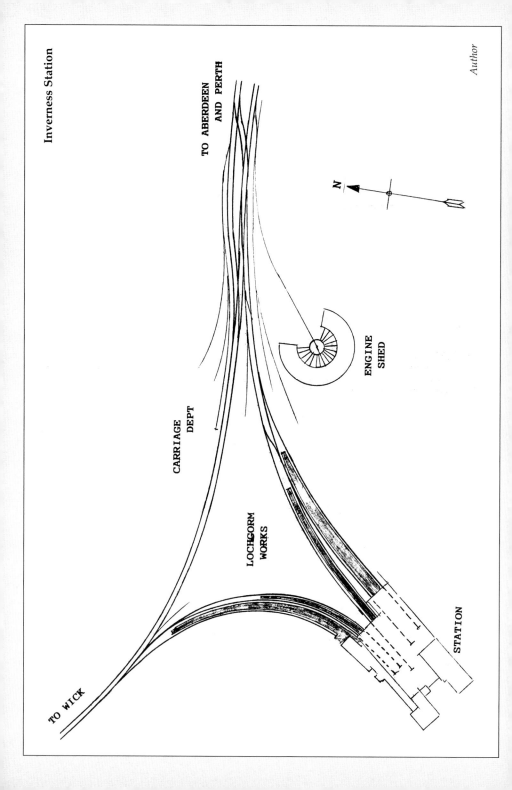

Inverness Station

TO ABERDEEN AND PERTH

CARRIAGE DEPT

ENGINE SHED

LOCHGORM WORKS

TO WICK

STATION

N

Author

As Dugald departed for his new job on the Highland Railway, his brother Peter, having completed his schooling, began an apprenticeship with Forrest & Barr, having expressed a desire to follow his older brother into the railway engineering sphere. The two brothers were now set into career paths which were eventually to result in them both attaining CME status with all the fame and recognition that was to be attached to that position.

Just over a couple of years were to elapse before Dugald was appointed Works Manager by Stroudley. His relationship with the Locomotive Superintendent was good and the works became an efficient organization under his management. The Highland Railway, at this time, was short of finance for new stock so Stroudley concentrated on rebuilding some existing singles into 2-4-0s. He made sure that the manufacture of the new parts was to a close tolerance, thus reducing the chance of excessive wear causing frequent calling-in for repairs. In this he had the competent assistance of Dugald who saw to it that the new or repaired parts were finished to a high quality. The resulting improvement in locomotive reliability soon proved its worth in the virtual elimination of poor timekeeping on trains. As the other types came into the works for servicing or overhaul similar quality techniques were applied in the reassembly. The HR, as a result of all this, became well-known for its reliability. Stroudley's only design to get built was an 0-6-0T which used many spare parts and reusable components found around the shops. Many have said this particular locomotive was the progenitor of the Brighton 'Terrier', but this is a very loose comparison; however, it did at least have the distinctive Stroudley domed cab roof and livery. So useful did this little locomotive prove that a further two appeared in 1872, by which time Stroudley had departed.

The advancement at Lochgorm works most certainly was welcome to Dugald and Jane, for now their family, eventually to be four sons and four daughters, had started to arrive with the first boy, George, on 18th August, 1866. However, the new arrival soon showed signs of illness and despite some 10 days of the best medical care available, died on 30th September from complications arising from a severe bronchial infection. Their home was rather basic, as was the norm for factory staff those days, and it must have been difficult for Jane to maintain a reasonable level of hygiene. The parents were devastated at this cruel loss and Dugald, after the funeral, immersed himself in the events at the works before going home to comfort his distraught wife.

By early 1867 Jane was pregnant again and almost a year after George's death, another baby boy arrived. Dugald's stubborn determination came through in his choice of name, again George, after his father. However, tragedy was to strike again in 1869 when this George died as an 11-month-old infant, but by this time he had a brother Walter who had been born on 24th May of that year. George's death certificate cites diarrhoea, so clearly matters in the home were still critical so far as hygiene was concerned. However, it is notable that Walter was born at a new address in Charles Street, so some action had been taken to get away from the basic conditions of the first home in Inverness. Additionally, Charles Street was much more convenient for the works, being only a short walk from the entrance.

For most of the years that Dugald was at Inverness the winters were harsh ones, with plenty of drifting snow causing problems on the railway. It was

Inverness engine shed *c*.1860s. The locomotive on the turntable is 2-2-2 No. 12 *Belladrum* built for the Inverness & Ross-shire Railway by Hawthorns of Leith.

No. 2 *Aldourie* was originally built by Hawthorns as a Barclay-designed 2-2-2 in 1855. Stroudley rebuilt it as a 2-4-0 in 1869 when Dugald was with him at Inverness. It lasted until 1899, being scrapped by Peter.   *Railway Magazine*

common for the HR to fit small snow ploughs to all locomotives in the depth of winter, but these could only cope with shallow drifts of up to two feet. Double-heading was often needed to cope with extremes greater than this. Stroudley, seeing the need for a range of ploughs to suit the particular conditions, designed three larger sizes, having them built in the works. The largest extended to the top of the smoke box and was used on the leading engine of a group of three or four coupled together to charge snow-drifts of up to 10 or 12 feet in depth.

Dugald was instrumental in the manufacture of these ploughs and also responsible for the shopping of locomotives such that they could be modified to take the range of ploughs in the minimum of time. In this, and other matters, Stroudley soon came to realise his Works Manager's worth in both production and modification matters.

The Highland Railway, formed in 1865 from the amalgamation of the Inverness & Aberdeen Junction and the Inverness & Perth railways, was still expanding in the late 1860s and early 1870s. The Dingwall & Skye Railway opened as far as Strome Ferry, being worked by the HR from the start. This particularly scenic route with a limited train service is, thankfully, still with us, and provides one of the few rail links to the west coast of Scotland north of the Clyde. There were several other lines projected to the western coast, namely Aultbea, Ullapool, Lochinver and Laxford Bridge. These, however, never came to fruition, for the sparse population could never have generated enough traffic to justify their construction.

Despite the moderate expansion of HR routes, finance for extra stock was still tight, and the lack of opportunity to flex his design muscles had Stroudley looking elsewhere for a more satisfying post. He found it in 1869, at the Brighton works of the London, Brighton & South Coast Railway (LB&SCR), who desperately needed a Locomotive & Carriage Superintendent to replace J.C. Craven upon his imminent retirement. Some 27 applications were received for this job and Stroudley secured it against some stiff competition.

After the departure of his chief to the South Coast of England, Dugald was briefly in total charge at Lochgorm, whilst the HR sought out a new Locomotive Superintendent. David Jones, who had been Stroudley's chief assistant, was eventually chosen. He and Drummond clearly did not get on too well, with Jones' daughter being on record as considering the Drummonds as being 'not socially acceptable'. This seems a harsh judgment on a family reeling from a double tragedy.

By this time Peter had completed his apprenticeship at Forrest & Barr and had moved to Messrs Norman and Co.'s engineering works in Glasgow to gain some more practical experience on the shop floor.

Some correspondence between Dugald and Stroudley clearly took place for, in early 1870, we find the former following his old chief to Brighton. Both he and Jane, with a very precious Walter, set off for the South Coast of England, leaving their sorrows in Inverness behind but not forgotten. They were not to return there for some 35 years, and then only for a family wedding.

However, the Drummond story at Inverness was not to finish with this departure for England, for upon Jones' resignation some 25 years later his successor was to be none other than Peter Drummond, but that episode will form part of the latter section of this book.

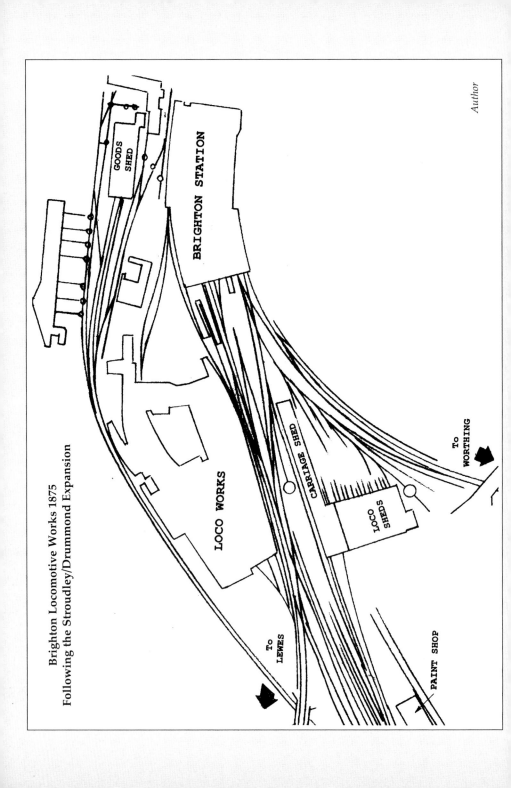

Brighton Locomotive Works 1875
Following the Stroudley/Drummond Expansion

GOODS SHED

BRIGHTON STATION

LOCO WORKS

CARRIAGE SHED

LOCO SHEDS

To LEWES

To WORTHING

PAINT SHOP

Author

Chapter Two

Brighton Days

The year 1870 was an important one in the annals of the LB&SCR. The Traffic Manager, J.P. Knight, was promoted to General Manager on 1st January of that year. His first major authorisation was the introduction of cheap workmen's tickets, following which he started planning for an acceleration in train services. The locomotive stock to accomplish this speeding up was a hotchpotch of largely obsolescent Craven types with little regard for commonality. At that time the LB&SCR had, it is recorded, no fewer than 72 classes of locomotive in service, hardly a recipe for economy and certainly a strain on maintenance!

Craven, the Locomotive Superintendent responsible for this act of non-standardisation, had indicated his intention of retiring at the end of 1869 and we have seen that Stroudley was appointed in his place. Craven, good engineer though he was, had never been outstanding on the production side and matters at the Brighton works, which awaited Stroudley's attention, were not very efficient as a result. Neither were the train services, for over the previous decade there had been a great increase in the lines and traffic which had not been matched by adequate improvements to the locomotive fleet and rolling stock. It was a similar sort of situation he had found upon his arrival on the HR. The LB&SCR Board clearly had done their homework well in sifting through the applications tendered, realising that it was not only a case of new design but of reorganization. The transformation at Inverness had not gone un-noticed.

Stroudley, after sizing up the situation and persuading Dugald to join him as Works Manager, decided that whilst reorganisazation was being planned his initial policy would be to rebuild some of the better Craven designs whilst letting the remainder gradually run down to scrapping, a move he rapidly obtained the Board's permission to implement. Simultaneously, he set the drawing office to scheming a new fleet of what was to become half-a-dozen new types having as much interchangeability as practicable.

The task facing Dugald upon his arrival in Brighton to rejoin Stroudley was to assist in the modernisation of the works from the somewhat disorganized situation. The main works were perched seemingly precariously on the eastern side of the hill overlooking London Road with little room for expansion, being flanked by the main line into Brighton station on the other, western, side. The station itself, plus the downhill slope beyond down to the seafront, blocked any growth in that direction and the northern confines were bordered by the curve of the line to Lewes and the east. So far as westward expansion was concerned, the steep slopes of the South Downs prevented anything in that direction, and that was on the other side of the main line anyway. Even with these restrictions, the space available was much more than there had been at the Lochgorm works of the HR. Brighton was a busy station, being a point where all trains from the London line had to reverse if going to Worthing. The Cliftonville spur permitting direct running did not open until 1879.

There were several major reorganizations needed at Brighton works when Stroudley and Drummond started their respective jobs. Firstly, to create more space for locomotive building, the carriage and wagon production was transferred from their original site on the western side of the main line. This permitted the existing locomotive depot, up to then part of the works, to be transferred to the west. This transfer of the spacious locomotive depot was possible now since the removal had taken place of the huge chalk hill which resulted from the depositing of spoil from the extensive cuttings and elsewhere on the Worthing and South Coast lines. A considerable area of land thus became available for use. The old erecting shop was turned into a smithy and a new one built. Up to that time the works had no foundry facilities and one was now incorporated. The paint shop was then moved out of the works to the western side of the line, north of the new locomotive department.

Dugald was to learn much for his future use in his later appointments on the North British Railway, Caledonian Railway (CR) and London & South Western Railway (LSWR) from his involvement in the Brighton reordering of Stroudley. Much of his future thinking in the context of works layouts was to benefit from this. Craven's wilderness of a disorganized works was soon to be transformed into an ordered and efficient place of production.

New design work was, however, initially minimal, the works reorganization taking priority. Dugald's management and organizational skills were much in demand to achieve this. The capacity of Brighton to turn out new locomotives was restricted by the extensive reordering and 12 of Stroudley's first design, an 0-6-0 goods engine, had to be ordered from Kitson & Co. to try and achieve their introduction into service in the required time. Two examples had already been turned out from Brighton works in 1871 and, after initial trials to iron out a few snags, proved their worth in traffic.

The 0-6-0, class 'C', was a keynote design to have a considerable impact on Dugald. Although the order for 12 had, in 1872, been placed on Kitson & Co., some last minute changes to the boiler caused some slippage in progress and delayed delivery quotes. Kitsons also had some difficulty in the casting of the cylinder blocks. Some production at Brighton therefore became a priority, with six more examples emerging from there in 1873. Dugald's initial reordering of the works played a great part in permitting the speedy deliveries of the 1873 batch of the class. They were, at the time, the largest goods engines of their kind in the British Isles, a fact which led to their eventual nickname of 'Jumbos'. The Kitson batch eventually started to arrive as the Brighton-built examples were being outshopped in 1873, with deliveries extending into 1874, to swell the class to 20.

Concurrent with the 1871 pair of 0-6-0s, Stroudley also built two 0-4-2Ts redesigned as side tanks from a Craven order for two double-framed saddle tanks for suburban passenger duties. He was already planning to introduce his own class 'D' 0-4-2Ts and these two examples were used to help develop the springing of the new design. This gave Dugald a good insight into the technicalities of front-coupled tanks, to be used to great effect by him later on.

Dugald watched and learnt from the design skills of his mentor. In his own locomotives in later years much of the engineering expertise of Stroudley was to be apparent. For example Stroudley was keen on any feature which could assist in economy of operation, coal being a relatively expensive item to a railway which had to transport all its supplies from collieries outside its area. One feature which could assist in reducing coal consumption was that of feed water heating, in which some of the waste heat of the exhaust steam was passed to the feed water.

However, there was a negative side to this in that, above a certain temperature of the feed, injectors would not function properly and it was necessary to resort to feed pumps. Stroudley continued to employ this method for many years, and it was one of his features that Dugald adopted for many of his own designs in the future. The feed-water heating was most certainly quite efficient, raising the temperature in the tanks sufficiently, in some cases, to blister the paint off the outside of the structure.

A year after Dugald's move to Brighton, brother Peter came to join him in a junior capacity, having recently completed his year of shop floor experience and decided that a career on the railways was definitely for him. A position was found for him as one of the foremen in the Running Department. He was to stay with Dugald for some years, to be much influenced and encouraged as his experience grew under the watchful eye of his elder brother.

By the time Dugald had made his presence felt in Brighton works, some of the shops were operating more efficiently and could begin to be set up for limited production (Craven, due to the restricted capabilities at Brighton, had tended to use private builders for much of the stock introduced by himself). The drawing office found itself at full stretch once the new types of locomotive were defined, and the works could now contemplate production of several classes simultaneously. The dependence on the private builders was dramatically scaled down, a fact which immediately had an effect on the cost of new locomotives. In fact, during the remainder of Stroudley's time only two batches of locomotives had to be ordered from private builders.

The home used by Dugald and his family was 21, Buckingham Road, which was located conveniently on the hill overlooking the terminus and just a short walk from the works. A short stroll from the house down Dyke Road and West Street would have brought them onto the promenade and beach. It was, indeed, a pleasant place to live and work.

So far as the furtherance of the family was concerned, the time at Brighton was blessed by three more children. The first was a daughter Christina in 1871, followed by another son George William in 1872, and then a second daughter Jane in 1875. Walter had plenty of company from now on. Both he and George were to become engineers at the urging of their father. Quite probably George's second name of William was in honour of Stroudley, who clearly had, by his actions after the Cowlairs fracas, enabled Dugald to have a second chance. The sorrows of Inverness were, to some extent, alleviated by this steady growth of the family.

By 1874 four classes, an 0-6-0, two types of 0-6-0T and an 0-4-2T were being turned out, some 273 locomotives in total being eventually added to the stock. The Brighton productivity had certainly benefited from the Stroudley/ Drummond input. Dugald's reputation as a competent Works Manager was beginning to spread. He also took advantage of his many meetings with Stroudley to study his design philosophy, locking away facts and features to be

LB&SCR Stroudley 'Terrier' No. 42 *Tulsehill*. *John Scott-Morgan Collection*

Eventually, the 'Terriers' could be found far away from Brighton. Here one is found on the Freshport, Yarmouth & Newport Railway on the Isle of Wight having come here from the LSWR Axminster-Lyme Regis branch. *Kenning Collection/John Scott-Morgan*

applied by himself in later years. Perhaps the most distinctive feature was Stoudley's penchant for the minimum number of holes in a boiler structure, which gave rise to dome mounted safety valves; this became the trademark of most Drummond boilers.

The smaller of the two 0-6-0Ts designed by Stroudley was the 'A' class, to become known as the 'Terrier', of which the first batch appeared in 1872 and remained in production until 1880, when the class totalled 50, whilst the 'D' class 0-4-2T was to be another popular engine, with some 125 eventually in service, built between 1873 and 1887. These particular designs were to influence the 0-6-0Ts and 0-4-4Ts emanating from Dugald in later years on other railways.

The second Stroudley 0-6-0T to appear was the 'E' class, for local goods and shunting work, the 'Terriers' having been aimed at light passenger operations. The first batch of six were turned out in 1874 with a further 72 appearing over the years up to 1891, so useful were they over the system. Some 30 lasted into British Railways (BR) days together with 10 that had been modified in Southern Railway (SR) days to 0-6-2T format to provide a light axle loading over some of the South Devon branches. The last survivor, BR No. 32694, was scrapped at Eastleigh in July 1961, after running some 1,524,493 miles, a huge figure for a locomotive that had spent much of its life on local goods and shunting work.

One further key change on the LB&SCR took place in 1875, this being the decision to adopt the Westinghouse brake as a standard on all fitted stock. George Westinghouse had visited Britain in 1871 to promote his invention of the air brake and several railways had shown interest, such that a series of braking trials to compare different systems were proposed by the Royal Commission on Railway Accidents. These duly took place at Newark in 1875, and the latest Westinghouse automatic brake resulted from these trials, being chosen by the LB&SCR, Great Eastern Railway, Caledonian Railway and North British Railway to be their standard. Dugald would have been involved in the early discussions at Brighton but by the time the choice was finally settled, he was elsewhere, as we shall see in the next Chapter. One of the locomotives provided for the trials was Stroudley's class 'B' 2-2-2, *Grosvenor*, which had been fitted experimentally with a Westinghouse vacuum brake system. This locomotive had been built with a steam brake which was most unpopular with the crew, who complained about it being fierce in operation. Trouble was also experienced with the vacuum system during the braking trials which convinced Stroudley to recommend the adoption of the Westinghouse air brake on the LB&SCR.

The days spent at Brighton had given both Dugald and Peter some very useful experience under Stroudley, whose excellent engineering expertise gave the brothers much sound practical knowledge for their respective futures, before an opportunity to move on came their way. Ever the immaculate and meticulous designer, Stroudley was saddened to lose the Drummond touch which had revolutionised the reorganization of the works. Despite their opposites in character with Stroudley, the brothers had been members of a good team which had, in a few brief years, lifted the output of the small Brighton works from mediocrity into an example of excellent engineering and reliability, the output of which was to serve through into the 20th century and on to Grouping.

Stroudley's ultimate express type, the 0-4-2 of class 'B', more generally known as the 'Gladstones'. No. 176 was built in 1890, one of the last batch of a long production run starting in 1883. *John Scott-Morgan Collection*

LB&SCR 4-wheel stock, built *c*.1880, remained in use for excursions almost up to Grouping. *John Scott-Morgan Collection*

Chapter Three

The Return to Scotland

By 1874 Dugald had designs on further advancement and, hearing that the North British Railway was looking for a new Locomotive Superintendent, applied for and obtained the position, taking office on 1st February, 1875. The previous incumbent, Thomas Wheatley, had, it seems, disagreed violently with some Board findings or instructions and resigned under somewhat of a cloud.

Now, the NBR had amongst its formative companies the Edinburgh & Glasgow Railway and had adopted that company's works at Cowlairs for its production and repair centre. However, Johnson had long since left Cowlairs and in 1873 was installed as Locomotive Superintendent on the Midland Railway (MR) at Derby, so there would be no adverse comment, or even blockage, of the return of Dugald from England. Ten years had passed since his outburst to Johnson and this previous misdemeanour had been forgotten.

The formation of the NBR system had put together a large and varied fleet of locomotives many of which were, by now, becoming obsolete. The expresses between Edinburgh and Glasgow were catered for by eight Beyer, Peacock single-drivers of 1856-61 vintage and most of the other goods and passenger services were hampered by the lack of powerful enough locomotives. The state of affairs was, concerning the locomotive stock, very similar to those encountered by Dugald on arrival at Brighton, and was certainly different to those existing during Dugald's previous time at Cowlairs. Some measure of standardisation was clearly needed to economise on operating costs, as was the modernisation and updating of the fleet.

Peter took little persuading to return to his homeland and came to the NBR with Dugald, this time in the position of foreman-erector, which really was a works assistant placing. His elder brother had ambitions for him and this position would place him on the ladder of promotion to, possibly, Works Manager and, eventually, Locomotive Superintendent. The brothers set to at Cowlairs to reorganize design and production matters.

It is in connection with this reorganization that we come across a clash of personalities affecting Dugald's position. The chairman of the Locomotive Committee was a Mr Muir, an elderly man who tended to keep keen youngsters in their place. Naturally, his ideas and forthright manner clashed with those of Dugald. Muir had backed all the improvements to Cowlairs works enthusiastically and expected all production of new stock to be placed there.

The express fleet was, Dugald decided, to be initially supplemented by a pair of 2-2-2s, class '474', which were almost straight copies, with a Drummond cab, of the Stroudley class 'B' 2-2-2 *Grosvenor* of 1874. This copy even sported a tender identical to the original of the Stroudley design, having under-hung springs to the wheels and the toolbox at the rear. Simultaneously, Dugald ordered the drawing office to design a goods 0-6-0 based on Stroudley's 'C' class. Both these new arrivals sported another feature copied from Stroudley, which was to become a Drummond trademark, in the form of safety valves

The Stroudley 2-2-2 *Grosvenor*, predecessor to a class of 24 2-2-2s of class 'G', built in 1874. This design was taken by Dugald to the NBR and used as the basis for a batch of two express locomotives for the Glasgow to Edinburgh services. About the only visible alterations were to the cab roof and provision of outside bearings to the tender wheels.   *Author's Collection*

Dugald Drummond's North British Railway 2-2-2 No. 474 of 1876.   *John Alsop Collection*

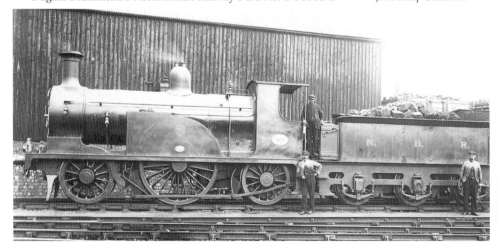

The Stroudley 0-6-0 class 'C'. No 421 of the 1873/4 Kitson batch.   *John Scott-Morgan Collection*

The first design of Drummond for the NBR, a copy of the Stroudley 'C' class 0-6-0. Thirty-two were built in 1876-1877, 20 by Neilson, 12 at Cowlairs. This is the last of the Neilson products of 1877.

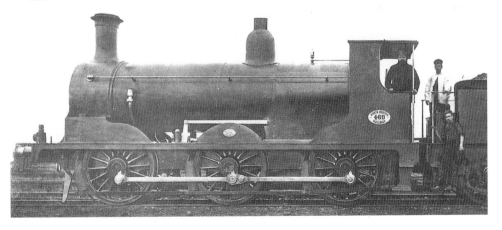

Drummond's '165' class 0-6-0T No. 49 at Carlisle Canal.   *John Alsop Collection*

'165' class 0-6-0T No. 108 at Perth with the cattle dock in the background.

John Alsop Collection

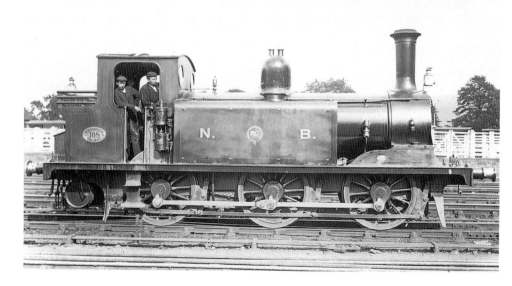

mounted on the dome. Of these 0-6-0s, class '100', a total of 32 were constructed by Cowlairs (12) and Neilson's of Glasgow (20).

The proposal that the production of 20 0-6-0s was to be placed with Neilson's was vigorously opposed by Muir on the grounds that, as mentioned above, the works was capable of building all locomotives required. However, after much acrimonious argument with Dugald, the Neilson order was confirmed but spread over two years, 1876 (12) and 1877 (8). But this episode had sown the seeds of dissent between Dugald and some of the Board members.

The two first excursions into designing indicated that he was determined to take no chances, and he followed the LB&SCR designs so strictly that one is tempted to postulate that he had been given permission to take with him sets of drawings of these, and other, locomotives when he left Brighton.

Coincident with the above additions, Dugald introduced an 0-6-0T, class '165', which was a clear copy of the Brighton 'Terrier', being only slightly larger in overall dimensions. Useful and popular little engines, the 25 constructed were to be found on local workings around Edinburgh and Glasgow, as well as on many branches, for many years, until displaced to shunting work in the early 1900s.

In May 1876 the through trains from St Pancras to Edinburgh commenced over the newly-constructed MR Settle to Carlisle line. The stock used for these included Pullman cars and Midland 12-wheeled coaches, the resulting train weights being much above those normal for the NBR. Coupled with this weight increase, the gradients on the NBR Waverley route between Carlisle and Edinburgh included lengthy stretches of up to 1 in 70 for as long as eight miles in both directions. The locomotives then available, the Wheatley '420' class 4-4-0s, were inadequate to maintain the timings on this route. Something more powerful was needed. Dugald's comment recorded about the NBR express engines at that time was succinct and to the point: 'Like skinny chickens, all legs and wings'. Clearly, some larger boilers were needed to improve the steaming for the large driving wheels powered by hungry cylinders.

Dugald had had an order placed with Neilson's for a batch of 20 of the 0-6-0s mentioned above and, once he had assessed the needs of the Waverley route, amended this order by substituting six of the 0-6-0s for four 4-4-0s, to be class '476', and the two singles mentioned earlier. But to the 4-4-0s. These were a complete departure from the Stroudley philosophy for express locomotives. That designer had steadfastly refused to condone leading bogies on any of his designs, and in fact was to hold fast on this principle to the end of his days. He was firmly of the opinion that leading driving wheels were perfectly satisfactory. Dugald's 4-4-0s were the first in a long line of his designs employing this wheel arrangement which were to grace British rails for much of the remainder of steam days. They followed Wheatley's pioneering designs in having inside cylinders, a feature which was to remain with all Drummond 4-4-0s whether designed by Dugald or Peter. Following some initial teething troubles associated with the cylinders, brakes and bogies they entered service in May 1877. They immediately proved capable of coping with the heavy expresses between Carlisle and Edinburgh. Double-heading was eliminated and the associated expense of this practice disappeared from the traffic returns.

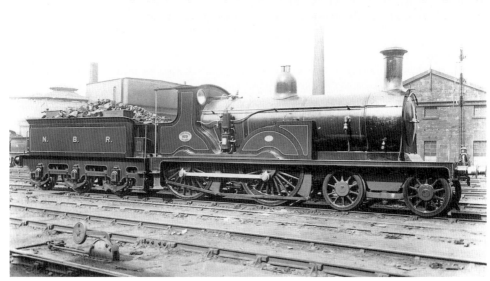

Drummond's '476' class 4-4-0 No. 479 built by Neilson in 1877 for the North British Railway.
John Alsop Collection

'476' class 4-4-0 No. 476. This locomotive remained in service until withdrawal in November 1924.
John Alsop Collection

The time at Cowlairs produced two more daughters for Dugald and Jane. The first, Janet, born on 12th March, 1878 and the second, Mary Winifred, born on 25th April, 1880. This completed the family which now comprised of two boys and four girls. Both girls were born at home, by then Cowlairs House, the official residence of the Locomotive Superintendent at 250, New Kippichill Road.

Peter, soon after his return to Scotland, became acquainted with Mary McKay Phillips. Their friendship grew closer and, after an engagement, they had married on 26th August, 1876 at the Maryhill Parish church and settled into a rented house on the Springburn Road, No. 415. It was not long before a cousin for Dugald's children appeared, for after a safe delivery at the Glasgow Royal Infirmary, on 28th January, 1878, Mary proudly returned home, which was now No. 6, Vulcan Road, with the first of three daughters, Jeanie Lennie.

Two small classes of tank locomotives appeared in 1877 and 1879. The first was an 0-4-2T based on the Stroudley class 'D', but slightly larger overall. It was given the class '157' designation. From the outset there were problems associated with the rear trailing axle, the weight on it proving a little excessive. Within a few years the entire class of six had been rebuilt as 0-4-4Ts and they spent much of their early days on passenger work. The next Drummond tank for the NBR was a 4-4-0T, class '494', which again was for passenger work. Three were built and had, for a tank locomotive of this type, large coupled wheels of 6 ft diameter.

Goods transit on the NBR represented a large part of the railway's traffic and in 1879 a new 0-6-0, class '34', somewhat lighter than the earlier 1876 design, appeared. They quickly became known as the 'Wee Drummonds' and a total of 101 were eventually to be constructed and found on many freight tasks. Again, like their larger predecessors, these locomotives followed Stroudley design principles. Of the 101, all were built at Cowlairs between 1879 and 1883, except for a batch of five from Dübs in 1879. To be based all over the NBR, many lasted after rebuilds in later years to enter London & North Eastern Railway (LNER) service at Grouping.

We have seen that it was his time at Brighton under Stroudley that set Dugald on the path of feed-water heating. The system used by Stroudley was basic and simple, that of passing exhaust steam into the tender or side tanks where it condensed and heated the water stored there. Until 1879 all Drummond locomotives for the NBR were provided with feed-water heating and pumps until, for some reason, all designs after that were fitted with injectors, beginning with the class '34' 0-6-0.

By now, it was clear that whilst Dugald had taken much of Stroudley's design aspects as his guidelines, his own thinking was starting to materialise. In the terms of that archetypical British express passenger locomotive, the 4-4-0, he was, in his time, to become perhaps one of the greatest exponents of this arrangement.

One person of importance to Dugald was that appointed chief draughtsman by him - one Robert Chalmers. Chalmers had been a draughtsman at Cowlairs during Dugald's first days there and was persuaded to join him at Brighton and spent five years there. One month after Drummond had settled in at Cowlairs,

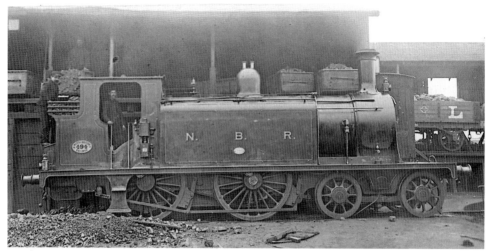

Drummond's '494' class 4-4-0T No. 494.   *John Alsop Collection*

'494' class 4-4-0T No. 494 once again. This locomotive was the first of the class built, in April 1879 and the last to be withdrawn as LNER 'D50' class No. 10390 in March 1926.

John Alsop Collection

Drummond '34' class 0-6-0 No. 128 at Burnbank in 1904.   *John Alsop Collection*

'34' class 0-6-0 No. 34.   *John Alsop Collection*

Chalmers returned to be given his chief draughtsman's post, which he held for 30 years thereafter, ending his time on the design of the NBR Atlantic in 1905-6.

Also, by now Dugald had Matthew Holmes as an assistant. Holmes had long been employed on the NBR and its predecessor the EGR. As rough and acrimonious was Dugald, Matthew Holmes was 'every inch a gentleman' who had considerable engineering gifts. As with Stroudley, Drummond got on with Holmes, recognising a competent assistant well capable of taking some of the, by now, considerable workload on his shoulders. Fireworks were not likely with such a person, and it was becoming clear that those with mild manners and an equable temperament were less likely to be drawn into disputes with a clearly forthright and overbearing personality. There was a downside to all this in that Dugald refused to be persuaded to adopt technical changes in the locomotive sphere. He always had to suggest any such matters himself, and his judgement in this, we shall see later, was sometimes questionable.

In 1875 the Association of Locomotive Engineers in Scotland had reconvened after a gap of some four years without meetings. At this meeting, on 12th November, Dugald Drummond was elected to membership to replace Wheatley. David Jones, now firmly established at Inverness on the HR, also joined the Association in place of founder member Stroudley, now well established and settled at Brighton. The only technical item recorded as being covered at this meeting appears to have been the costing of wagon repairs. Following this hesitant start to affairs the Association went into abeyance, to be reformed in later years as the Association of Railway Locomotive Engineers (ARLE), when it expanded to cover Great Britain and Ireland, setting itself to 'meet twice a year to discuss matters of interest to Railway Engineers and Railway Companies'. Both Dugald and Peter were to be involved in this body in later years, as we shall see in later Chapters.

Peter, meanwhile, was gradually climbing through the works management hierarchy, making sure that he supported his brother's endeavours to run an efficient design and production organization. Although not quite as abrasive as Dugald in his handling of the workforce, he was, of course, treated with the utmost caution by them. The Drummond strict discipline and forthright manner was very much a way of life at Cowlairs, as witness the times when Dugald's rough manner and resolute action sometimes resulted in the works employees being pushed to their limits of acceptance. Despite this they realised that here was a good organizer of their tasks fully conversant with their procedures, having gone through the shop floor himself earlier. Doubtless he had a good cause to implement in order to trim costs or introduce new techniques on the shop floor, but his instructions were sometimes too blunt and direct for them to stomach. He expected immediate acquiescence and any departure from his instructions were swiftly dealt with. As regards discipline, the breaking of rules was not condoned at all, as when a foreman was caught smoking on duty and summarily dismissed. Clearly this was a popular foreman, for the erecting shop men downed tools and walked out on strike. When Dugald was around the men had to watch their 'ps and qs'. Many of them must have heaved a sigh of relief in 1882 when he resigned to take up the Locomotive Superintendency of the Caledonian Railway.

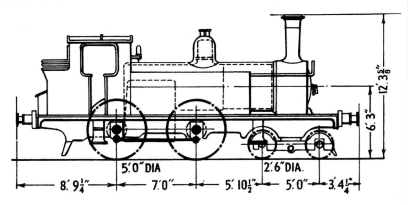

Thirty of these 4-4-0Ts, class '72' were built for suburban and branch line use between 1880 and 1884. They were distinguished by their bogie disc wheels.

Dugald's last design for the NBR was a 4-4-0T, class '72', of which 30 were built between 1880 and 1884. These were a smaller version of his earlier 1879 4-4-0T passenger tank of which just three had been built. They were notable for their disc wheels on the bogie and such was their usefulness some of them lasted 50 years, truly significant of a sound design. Mostly used for suburban work for many years, some eventually were drafted out to branch line work on which they ended their days.

As regards outside interests, Dugald was elected a Member of the Institution of Civil Engineers on 31st May, 1881. Also, as regards his boys, Walter had begun his schooling in 1875, being sent to the Albany Academy, the school attached to Glasgow University. He would have received a sound education at this prestigious establishment. George joined his brother at the Academy in 1878. Clearly Dugald was determined to give his sons the best academic start possible.

With a rapidly growing reputation and the locomotive fleet of the NBR being improved by the addition of a wide range of types for all duties, events seemed destined for Dugald to be settled for many more years at Cowlairs. However, in mid-1882 the NBR Board minutes stated: 'The resignation of Mr Drummond, Locomotive Superintendent, is reported'. He left on 27th July, 1882 for the Locomotive Superintendency of the Caledonian Railway at St Rollox Works, a place as yet unfamiliar with the Drummond ways. It has been suggested that it was the salary increase obtained of £700, to £1,700 (about £200,000 in today's terms), proved the lure to drag Dugald away from a steady job. However, the briskness of the Board minutes comment gives the impression of something else having caused the move. Maybe the outspoken Dugald had commented on some matter too harshly at a Locomotive Committee meeting, he was never renowned for being diplomatic. Perhaps the following might throw some light on the causes.

Dugald's standing with the Board of the NBR was much damaged during the Board of Trade inquiry into the Tay Bridge disaster. One theory propounded was that the train had derailed and that had caused a critical structural failure which had brought down the bridge. This was forthrightly attacked by Dugald as being totally incorrect and put over in blunt terms in court as a whitewash.

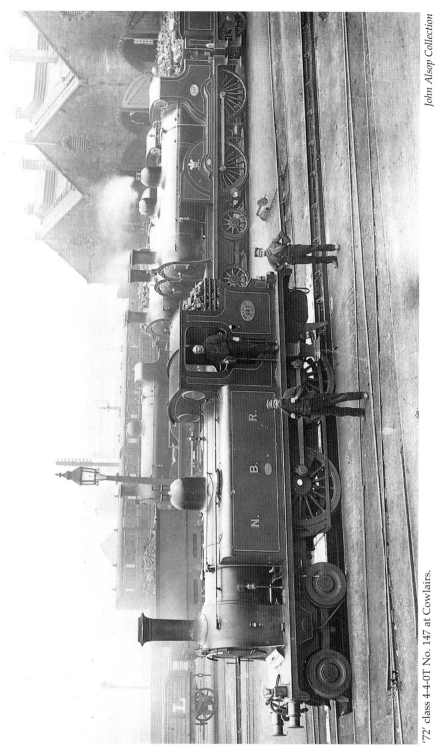

'72' class 4-4-0T No. 147 at Cowlairs.

Furthermore, his opinion of Bouch, the bridge designer and builder, was not high and many criticisms were flung at the unfortunate engineer during the inquiry. The Board's opinion of Bouch was clearly not in line with that of Dugald, and a permanent rift appeared, which was never healed.

It was not surprising that matters eventually came to a head over an apparent discrepancy in some accounts connected with the disposal of old timber from the carriage and wagon department. In June 1882 Dugald was asked to explain this and he duly submitted a report. What followed was never fully explained, for the reasons that follow. Firstly, it was not until Drummond had left that his successor, Holmes, and the stores superintendent were instructed to enquire and submit their analysis of his report. Secondly, the September locomotive and stores committee meeting put off the consideration of this analysis until the following meeting. Thirdly, at this next meeting, at which the Chairman and five Directors were present, although entered in the minutes book, no minutes were taken, the only item which appears is a pencilled note 'No minute written by chairman'. This was the only un-minuted meeting of any committee the NBR held during the whole of its existence. Fourthly, there is no surviving General Manager's copy letter book for October 1882. A cover-up? Maybe, for Dugald may have been very forthright and outspoken, but definitely not underhand or deceitful. And besides, what railway company of the standing of the Caledonian would offer a top job to anyone whose integrity was questionable?

One legacy left on the NBR by Dugald was the Westinghouse air brake. In December 1876 he had organized some trials with this system which resulted in it being adopted as a standard feature from then on. Other nearby railways also participated in these trials.

Peter, meantime, stayed on in his works assistant's post, preferring, for the time being, to further his ambitions without the continual presence and influence of Dugald.

'72' class 4-4-0T No. 225 at Fort William. *John Alsop Collection*

Dugald Drummond in 1884.   *The Baillie*

Chapter Four

Caley Days

On arrival at St Rollox, Dugald immediately took stock of the locomotive and works' situations. The locomotive stock of the CR was in a worse state than that of the NBR had been before he took office on that railway. There was a small sprinkling of 4-4-0s, but the vast majority of types consisted of 2-4-0, 0-4-2 tender types and 0-4-4Ts, all relatively small engines and mostly outside-cylindered. As a short-term measure some of the existing stock was reboilered by Dugald whilst he sized up the needs of replacements, impressing on the Board that a major programme of scrap and build was required.

In 1882 the CR adopted the Westinghouse air brake as standard on the recommendation of Drummond following its satisfactory application on the NBR. Some stock had already been fitted with it following the 1876 trials and Dugald was able to persuade the Board to release funds to complete the work.

The drawing office was ordered to start scheming an 0-6-0 goods type and an express 4-4-0. To be employed in this office shortly was a clearly competent draughtsman, R.W. Urie, who in the future was to play a key role with Dugald in England. The ability of Urie did not go unnoticed, for Dugald was, like so many eminent engineers of his ilk, constantly on the look out for bright junior men for the future, particularly those who would be able to take complete responsibility for work delegated their way.

Once design matters were under way he began to bring St Rollox works up-to-date and ensuring that, in future, much of the future production needs could be dealt with there. Whilst this was taking place, when the 0-6-0 and 4-4-0 designs were complete, orders totalling 35 and 10 respectively were placed with nearby Neilson's, to ensure a speedy entry into service of the sorely needed engines.

The 4-4-0s, of classes '66', of which 29 were built up to 1891, and '13' for the six built thereafter, were a welcome addition for the Carlisle to Glasgow expresses from Euston with their heavy London & North Western Railway (LNWR) stock. They eliminated most of the double-heading and enabled the service to be accelerated. Such was their success that in 1885 Dübs & Co. of Glasgow asked for, and received, permission to build one example to display at the 1886 Edinburgh Exhibition, at which it was subsequently awarded a gold medal. This exhibition example was initially fitted with Bryce-Douglas valve gear which was based on marine practice. However, this experiment was not successful and within a year it had been replaced by conventional link motion. Purchased by the CR after the exhibition it was put on the Ardrossan services and was unusual for a Caledonian locomotive in being named. That chosen was *Eglington*, after the Earl who owned most of Dugald's birthplace. They were to become the premier Drummond express 4-4-0s on the CR, although the six class '13' were not built under Dugald, but appeared largely unchanged during McIntosh's days, such was their outstanding performance. The first 10 of the '66s' were contracted out to Neilson's, the remainder, except for the Dübs

Drummond's class '66' No. 1069 at Carlisle (Kingmoor).   *John Alsop Collection*

Class '66' 4-4-0 No. 90 in immaculate condition at Perth.   *John Alsop Collection*

'66' class No. 66 at Carlisle. It is seen here after rebuilding with a 'Dunalistair' boiler.

John Alsop Collection

Although sporting a domed boiler with safety valves in the conventional position, class '13' 4-4-0 No. 17, built under Lambie, is pure Drummond and otherwise identical to the class '66'.

'294' class 0-6-0 No. 200 at Dundee West. *John Alsop Collection*

'711' class 0-6-0 No. 712 at Dundee West. *John Alsop Collection*

exhibition example, were all St Rollox products. It was on these designs that a new front end was embodied which enhanced their overall performance. All the steam passages were made as short as possible, for Dugald realised that long, sometimes tortuous, passages produced further losses on steam chest pressure of the steam entering the cylinders. He repositioned the steam ports at the ends of the valve face whilst the slide valves themselves were divided, each half being given its own exhaust port. These exhaust ports were split horizontally into upper and lower areas with the steam of the lower area passing through passages around the outside of the cylinders. All his future 4-4-0s which employed slide valves were to follow this pattern of front end design which provided free-running and economical characteristics.

The 0-6-0, classes '294' and '711', was destined to become the largest type, totalling 224, built under Dugald and had been designed in record time, for the first batch, from Neilson's, was ordered just four months after his arrival at St Rollox. It was based on the Drummond NBR class '34' and like that design was a sturdy, simple and reliable locomotive with a wide range of duties. The 0-6-0s took time to grow to this sizeable fleet as their production, all at St Rollox save the Neilson batches, was spread over the 12 years until 1897, and were kept in production by Smellie, Lambie and McIntosh. They all had long lives, the earliest withdrawal taking place in 1946 and the last example not disappearing until 1963. Eventually dubbed 'Jumbos' they were to be found all over the railway system in Scotland after Grouping, even displacing similar, but younger, types of the other railways.

Following these initial goods and express types came a small 0-4-4 passenger tank, class '171', specifically to replace some antiquated examples of obsolete motive power found on some of the branch lines. Twenty-four were built at St Rollox between 1884 and 1891.

So far as other tank engines were concerned, four more classes appeared, three of them saddle tanks. The first was a batch of two 0-4-2STs of class '262' built especially for the Killin Railway, which opened to traffic on the 1st April, 1886. This little 5½ mile branch leading down to Loch Tay operated as an independent company until 1923. For many years the 'wee train', as the locals dubbed it, was catered for by these little tanks.

Next came the first pair of 0-4-0STs of class '264' for general shunting duties, primarily around docks, for which they were almost exclusively employed. Thirty-five in all were turned out between 1885 and 1908. Dugald actually had little to do with the 0-4-0ST as it was primarily a Neilson design with sundry of his features such as chimney, smokebox and cab fittings. This explains why outside cylinders were tolerated on these locomotives. He could not justify the expense of changing to inside cylinders in the interest of interchangeability between these and some earlier outside-cylindered 0-4-0STs already in service when he arrived.

By 1885, Dugald has established himself well at St Rollox and was making a name for himself and decided, or was persuaded by his equivalents on other railways, to apply for Membership of the Institution of Mechanical Engineers. The list of sponsors on the application form is impressive: William Adams (LSWR); J.C. Park, North London Railway (NLR); S.W. Johnson (MR); W. Dean,

Class '171' 0-4-4T No. 193 at Perth. *John Alsop Collection*

Class '171' 0-4-4T No. 223 still in CR livery *c.*1924/5. *R.S. Carpenter Collection*

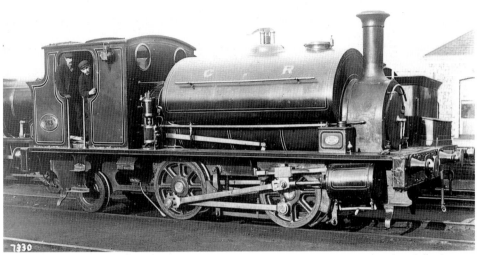

Class '262' 0-4-2ST No. 263 of 1885.   *John Alsop Collection*

Ex-CR class '262' 0-4-2ST, of which only two were built in 1885, still extant in Inverness on 27th
May, 1947, its twin No. 15000 having been withdrawn in 1928.   *J.M. Jarvis.*

Class '264' 0-4-0ST No. 617 inside Dalry Road shed, Edinburgh. *John Alsop Collection*

This class '264' 0-4-0ST was one of a dozen examples which lasted into BR days. It eventually became the St Rollox works pilot until being sent south to Crewe works. This photograph dates from April 1952 at St Rollox. *R.S. Carpenter Collection*

Great Western Railway (GWR). The inclusion of Samuel Johnson is interesting, for clearly the bad feeling that had ensued from the 1865 incident at St Rollox was forgotten and he and Dugald were reconciled. In fact, in later years Johnson was to sponsor Peter, Walter and George Drummond in their respective I.Mech.E. applications.

Two years later, in 1887, appeared his penultimate tank design for the CR, an 0-6-0ST of class '385'. This locomotive was quite unlike earlier Drummond designs so far as the cab was concerned. This was similar to a Stirling single bent sheet type. It also had the inside cylinders preferred by Dugald. Despite the poor protection this cab offered to the crew, a total of 30 were built and employed on shunting work previously undertaken by elderly time-expired four-coupled tender engines. This class quickly became known as 'Jubilee Pugs' due to the year of their design, that of Queen Victoria's Golden Jubilee.

With the works reorganization well under way, and the workforce coming to terms with the strict regime ordered by Dugald, and considerable publicity arising from the vastly improved motive power on the Caledonian, local publications sought interviews with the Locomotive Superintendent. As regards Dugald's dealings with those he came into contact with outside the railway environment, he always appeared approachable once they had got used to his sharp manner. This sharpness was compared by some to a rather imperious nature, yet, behind this was discerned a genuine and honest person. He had, after all, risen through the ranks to his top position and the rough Lowland background still showed through.

In 1886 there appeared a unique locomotive, the Caledonian 'Single'. There has been much argument about the genesis of this type. Neilson's of Glasgow had a line drawing of a proposed exhibition engine for the Edinburgh Exhibition of 1886, which at first sight appeared to be a Drummond design, as the boiler mountings were typical of his style. This locomotive was an outside-cylindered single-driver with 8 ft 3 in. wheels and was similar in concept to the Great Northern Railway (GNR) Stirling 8 ft Single. The CR Board having indicated that they would have no objection to this proposal being given Caledonian livery, then suggested that they would like to be the eventual exhibitor at Edinburgh, as they would be for the 4-4-0 mentioned earlier. What Dugald's comments were when acquainted with this proposal is not known, but his influence was certainly felt. Outside cylinders, so far as he was concerned were not acceptable and the huge drivers were soon reduced to a more acceptable 7 ft. The cylinders and motion were to be as for the '66' class 4-4-0.

As with the No. 124 4-4-0, this Single was awarded a gold medal and, following the closure of the Exhibition, was purchased by the CR and put into service on the Edinburgh to Carlisle line, being given the class '123' designation. In the race to Edinburgh of August 1888 this locomotive achieved a remarkable time on the 106.6 miles from Carlisle to Edinburgh. The load was only 80 tons, comprising four 8-wheeled coaches, and was conveyed over that distance in a mere 102 minutes and 33 seconds. When allowing for the lengthy gradients on this run, it was an excellent performance. Surprisingly this solitary locomotive survived into London Midland & Scottish Railways (LMS) days, being preserved by that railway as a static museum piece in the 1930s. Today it is to

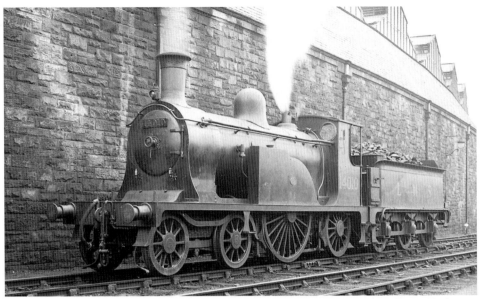

The Drummond Single No. 123 escaped scrapping to come back into ordinary traffic in 1930 for five years, working between Perth and Dundee. Here in LMS crimson lake livery it is found at Perth on 17th April, 1933.   *R.G. Jarvis/MRT*

Drummond 'Caley' Single in preserved condition looking resplendent in Caledonian Railway livery.

be found in the Glasgow Museum of Transport, the sole survivor of a Dugald Drummond pattern Scottish locomotive.

The final tank design to come from Dugald's time on the CR was to be an 0-6-0ST, class '272', which was basically a stretched version of the earlier class '264' 0-4-0ST. Six were built in 1888, and were distinguished by the scanty cab similar to that fitted to the larger 0-6-0ST of the previous year.

One particular feature introduced during Drummond's time on the CR was the 'Caley' hooter in place of the normal whistle. This latter was of a particularly shrill sound, which could best be described as a shriek. The distinctive mellow tone of the replacement carried well and was to be perpetuated on the locomotives of that railway for the rest of its existence, and was eventually to be adopted by Stanier when he became CME of the LMS.

The workload for the simultaneous reorganization of the works and design of new locomotives was very high. We have seen that Dugald was very dictatorial on shop floor matters and clearly needed a reliable person to whom to delegate much of the works' affairs. He waited for an opportunity to insert Peter into the works management area, achieving this in 1888. He still had high hopes for Peter and this placing was, we shall see, eventually to set events into order for the achievement of a Locomotive Superintendency for his brother.

Whilst all the re-stocking of the CR with new and improved locomotives had been taking place Peter and Mary had increased their family by a further two girls, Christina Thomson being born on 12th March, 1884 and Elsie on 24th July, 1888. By this time the family was living at 17, Petershill Road.

In 1884, having completed his education at the Albany Academy, Walter was apprenticed under his father at St Rollox works. It was a slightly unorthodox apprenticeship of six years, with one of those years spent in France at the works of the Chemin de Fer de l'Ouest in Paris, from where he returned in 1890 to find his father *en route* to Australia. George, meantime, had also been apprenticed at St Rollox since 1886. Clearly, Dugald was determined to have his sons in the railway sphere.

In 1888 at the Institution of Civil Engineers a paper on compound locomotives was read which produced some considerable interest. Dugald took note of the report on this paper and, in addition to his task of overseeing the design of locomotives for service on the CR, approached the Directors for authority to build a compound type to test the merits of such a locomotive as compared to similar simple expansion designs. In his interest to provide all means of economy, he felt that here was a worthwhile research task. Elsewhere, compounds were appearing, not only as prototypes but as production items and proving relatively successful. This request for research funds was refused and so he decided to test the effects of employing higher boiler pressures on the current designs. A series of test at pressures of 150, 175 and 200 psi proved that this pressure increase was worthwhile, provided that the locomotives were driven expansively; i.e. with full open regulator and a relatively short cut-off setting. Unfortunately these tests coincided with his resignation and the drivers were never impressed on the advantages available and reverted to their old established practice of partial regulator and wider cut-off. Coincident with this was an improvement in front end design as, in conjunction with the boiler

'385' class 0-6-0ST No. 399 at Perth.   *John Alsop Collection*

'80' class 4-4-0 No. 82 at Gourock with a boat train in 1907.   *John Alsop Collection*

pressure exercise, he had instigated a number of changes to the steam admission and exhaust ports of the slide valves.

This latter decision was fortuitously employed on the final batch of Drummond 4-4-0s, the class '80', for the CR outshopped from St Rollox in 1888. Basically, this was a smaller variant of the '66' class. Six appeared in 1888, to be followed by a similar batch in 1891. These latter six were ordered by Drummond's successor, Smellie, who made several changes to the boiler. The net result was a very free-running and economical class of locomotives.

In 1889 a series of tests between Edinburgh and Carlisle with these new 4-4-0s, at boiler pressures listed above gave the results Dugald had hoped for, that higher boiler pressures used in conjunction with expansive working, produced results nearly as good as that anticipated from a compound. In this year Dugald had obtained funding to carry out these tests. For this he selected four of the latest batch of class '66', Nos. 76 to 79. Nos. 76 and 79 had their boilers pressed to 200 psi, Nos. 77 and 78 set to 175 and 150 psi respectively. These locomotives were successively rostered for working the 10.15 am Edinburgh to London express as far as Carlisle, from where they returned on the 4.30 pm London to Edinburgh service. This was a smartly timed service, calling for average speeds of 51.35 mph on the down run and 50.08 mph on the up run.

The locomotives were also fitted with indicating gear which enabled the indicated horse power (ihp) to be measured, a maximum value of 1,238 ihp being recorded on No. 79, which was equivalent to a mean effective pressure (mep) of 940 hp. No mean power output bearing in mind the date.

The findings in terms of fuel savings due to the employment of higher pressures were as follows: No. 77 (175 psi) showed a 15 per cent reduction in fuel consumption over No. 78 (150 psi), whereas No. 76 (200 psi) gave a 31 per cent reduction over No. 78 and 11.92 per cent over No. 77. Johnson on the MR had also carried out some similar tests employing higher boiler pressures and shown that an increase from 140 psi to 160 psi produced a fuel saving of 11 to 13 per cent, broadly in line with Dugald's tests on the CR.

The report of these test results was eventually to be submitted to the Institution of Civil Engineers (ICE) and given as a paper, entitled *An Investigation into the Use of Progressive High Pressures in Non-Compound Locomotive Engines*, in 1897. The clear, concise, way in which it was presented obtained Dugald the award of the ICE Telford Medal in 1898. The CR really gained nothing from all this, other than a clear indication of the benefits of higher boiler pressures, for by the time the results had been analysed, Dugald was no longer around to implement the findings in practice. However, as Churchward found nearly 15 years later, good steam passages combined with high pressures and expansive working could offer equivalent economies to a compound. Dugald certainly had a good grasp of the way things should go to improve the overall performance of the steam locomotive. However, before any further steps could be taken along those lines, fate was to intervene from an entirely unexpected region.

As the end of the 1880s approached, the Association of Railway Locomotive Engineers was reformed, this time expanded to cover all the railways in England, Scotland, Ireland and Wales, the first meeting being held on 30th

October, 1889. Those present at this venue were Stirling, South Eastern Railway (SER), Stroudley (LB&SCR), J.C. Park, North London Railway, and Hanbury (Metropolitan). Unable to attend were Adams (LSWR); Kirtley, London, Chatham & Dover Railway (LCDR); Holden, Great Eastern Railway (GER); Johnson (MR) and Drummond (CR). In their absence Johnson and Drummond were elected Chairman and Vice-Chairman, with James Stirling becoming Secretary and Treasurer. Twice-yearly meetings were proposed, to be held in January and June.

The first summer meeting took place on 13th June, 1890, and the members attending the venue at the Royal Hotel, Edinburgh, were saddened by the recent death of Stroudley who had suffered pneumonia following a severe chill caught in France during some trials of one of his 'Gladstone' 0-4-2s on the French railways. Dugald would have been particularly saddened at this loss of a good friend, who had stood firmly behind him and shown understanding in time of trouble and had also been such an influence on his own design philosophy. Those present also paid tribute to Dugald, who had shortly before set sail for Australia and a new position.

It is at this point the careers of the Drummond brothers were to diverge, after they had worked closely together for some 20 years. Dugald took the opportunity overseas whilst Peter, now a senior assistant on the Works Manager's staff at St Rollox, remained there, awaiting fairly inevitable future promotion. From this point on the story of Dugald and Peter will diverge, with the former's career being covered first.

A Drummond rebuild of a Brittain CR 4-4-0s of 1877. No. 125 is *en route* to Ardrossan, Dugald's birthplace.   *John Scott-Morgan Collection*

Chapter Five

Disaster Down Under

In the early 1890s an episode involving Dugald emigrating took place. This has been very briefly referred to in other publications, but the details surrounding what took place leading up to and during that event have never been published. Some research into the happenings in Australia has, however, enabled the main events to be discovered and, as they constitute the beginning of a major turning point in Dugald's career, the story so far unearthed is incorporated in this Chapter.

Just as politics did, and still do, play an important part in the fortunes of industry this side of the World, so they have in the extremities of the British Empire. The story begins with the growth of an Australian engineering company, Hudson Brothers, which had expanded into work associated with the many railways then thrusting into and across the vast island continent.

Hudson Bros had an engineering factory built in 1882 and sited at Granville, New South Wales (NSW), which lies in an area near Sydney. This area was unofficially known as New Glasgow because of the large number of immigrants from Scotland who had settled there. From the start this company proved quite prosperous, recording a first year profit of £30,363 9s. 9d. The shareholders were to receive a dividend of 10 per cent from this, clearly, good start to the new enterprise.

Hudson Bros, in building up its engineering expertise, had recruited many of the Scottish immigrants with the appropriate skills, in particular encouraging their retention by making company houses available. These skilled workers formed the backbone of the engineering staff at the Granville works, bringing with them the expertise from old established industries that flourished in Glasgow and the other areas of Scotland. Much of the early railway work of the company was increasingly involved in the provision of rolling stock for the growing Australian railway network.

Matters took a turn for the worse in 1886, in that orders for the rolling stock began to taper off, resulting in half the workforce having to be laid off. Henry Hudson, the eldest of the four brothers running the company, applied himself to the stemming of this loss of orders by envisaging the setting up of a great locomotive works from which he foresaw a steady output for not only the New South Wales railways, but the entire railway system throughout the Australian Continent. With the backing of other local industries, in 1887 he tendered for the supply of 50 locomotives to the New South Wales Railways. There followed repeated representation to the Government authorities, who eventually stated their willingness to consider proposals for the setting up of a concern to do this. Hudson booked a passage on the first available ship for England on a fact-finding mission, setting sail in November 1889.

Reaching London, he found, in the City, several interested parties willing to consider backing him, and commenced on a tour of locomotive facilities. By the end of March 1890 news got through to the Sydney press that Hudson had formed, in London, the 'Australasian Locomotive Engine Works Company Limited' and had found a locomotive engineer of repute who would be the Managing Director in Sydney. This combination of Australian enterprise and British capital he confidently expected to employ 1,000 men and be in receipt of orders from the NSW Government for locomotives totalling some 75 per year for at least five years.

During his short time in the UK he clearly had sought out some expertise on the locomotive side of affairs, realising that an experienced man would be needed to put all his plans in order. Obviously, he had contact with locomotive builders in the UK and visited some of them to see for himself what was involved at first hand. What was urgently needed were some key people with the necessary experience in organizing and running a locomotive works. In addition, if that person could also take charge of the design matters, this would be a bonus. Someone with the knowledge and experience of a Locomotive Superintendent, who also had an extensive workshop experience, would have to be found and offered the chance to come to Australia. It is not too difficult to reason why he was drawn to Scotland in his search. With so many Scottish immigrants employed back in Australia he would have a good grasp of their capabilities. Also, in and around Glasgow were a clutch of locomotive works, both private and those belonging to some of the railways.

Within a short time of investigating locomotive production methods, Hudson met up with Dugald. Exactly how this meeting came about is not clear, but certainly he realised that here was a straight-talking and abrasive individual who clearly got things done with the minimum of argument, and a Scotsman who should have no difficulty in handling his large contingent of Scottish immigrant workers. Also, Dugald's prowess as a locomotive designer was there for all to see, operating on the CR. Hudson accordingly offered Dugald the position of Managing Director of his fledgling company, with the express remit of setting up the production of locomotives designed in house.

The offer must have been a generous one, and well paid, to persuade Dugald to relinquish his steady, established, post at St Rollox. These works had been completely reorganized and he now had several of his designs in series production at that time. However, the lure of Hudson's carrot was enough to tempt Dugald and, in mid-1890, he resigned his Caledonian position and set sail for his new posting. The Caledonian Railway was now in a good motive power position, so the resignation of its Locomotive Superintendent could be accepted without much disruption to its affairs. Just before he left the British Isles for 'down under', he sent a farewell message to his colleagues in the ARLE at their summer meeting at the Royal Hotel in Edinburgh. He had been the Vice-Chairman for the previous year and his forthright comments were missed by some. The Minutes of the ARLE state that those present recorded their thanks for his work connected with that organization.

Upon his arrival in Sydney, Dugald found the new company without an order on the books and the New South Wales Government setting up a group of three Commissioners to run the New South Wales Railways Department. Committees, for that was what this arrangement in essence was, can rarely be speedy in their deliberations, and this one was no exception. Orders promised never materialised and the whole scheme for quantity production of locomotives by the company began to collapse.

The railway scene in and around Sydney employed some interesting examples of motive power, some of which would have been very familiar to Dugald. For some of the passenger trains on the Sydney suburban traffic were hauled by 0-6-0Ts which were almost a direct copy of the Stroudley 'Terrier'. The New South Wales Railway had a total of eight, all built locally, which had been in service since their construction in 1875 by Mort & Co (4) and Vale & Lacey (4). The only departure from Stroudley's design was in the cab and bunker, the former more open and airy to suit the warmer climate and the latter larger to cope with the lower quality fuel available.

Dugald's comments on the situation concerning the non-appearance of the orders would have been direct and blunt, diplomacy never being one of his attributes, and by the early days of 1891 he announced his intention of returning to Scotland. Thus, a little over a year after arriving in Australia he set sail for home. Even the straight-talking Australians must have breathed a sigh of relief as he departed their shores.

Hudson Brothers continued in business until 1898, when it was wound up and absorbed by the Clyde Engineering Company, Henry Hudson becoming a leading light in that company. Ironically, Clyde Engineering was, from the first decade of the 20th century, to become a major supplier of locomotives and rolling stock to the Australian railways. Today, as part of the Evans Deakin Industries Group, it is very much involved in supplying the same to the modernised railway companies. Henry Hudson's dream had, eventually, been realised.

Clearly, whilst in Australia, Dugald did involve himself in some preliminary design studies of locomotives, and probably had some drawings of his Scottish designs with him. An examination of photos of the early locomotives to appear later, under Clyde Engineering auspices, reveals a distinctive Drummond chimney. This, and other features, particularly marine big ends and very sturdy construction, were the legacy left in Australia to remind people of what might have happened much earlier had circumstances been different. The first locomotives to emerge from Clyde Engineering works were a batch of 30 freight 2-8-0s for the New South Wales Railways. Together with these freight types was an order for a batch of 30 passenger locomotives. They all had the Drummond features mentioned above and, to crown it all, bogie tenders. Production started in 1907 and in May of that year Henry Hudson watched the first of the initial batch of four on its trial run. A week later, with the realisation of a dream made true, he died.

Upon Dugald and the family's return from Australia, they settled into Glaswegian life at No. 180, Bath Street. Brother Peter was still at St Rollox climbing the ladder in works managership. Dugald also insisted on his father, now retired from his railway inspector's post, coming to live with them as he had spent some 12 years alone since his wife Christina had died in 1879 and, at the age of 76, needed some extra care. Dugald may have been a difficult and cantankerous person at work, but he certainly took care of his family at home.

The New South Wales Railways version of the Stroudley 'Terrier'. This is the last of eight produced in 1880 for suburban services around Sydney. It was withdrawn in 1893 and sold to a contractor, not being finally scrapped until 1940.   *ARHS/(NSW) Railway Resource Centre*

This 2-8-0 of class 'T', for the New South Wales Railway shows distinctive Drummond features, notably the chimney, marine bearings and 8-wheel tender. This is the first production version of the Clyde Engineering Co. batch of 1907-8. Withdrawn in 1965 it is now preserved.
ARHS/(NSW) Railway Resource Centre

He was not badly off, despite the year's absence abroad, and there was sufficient capital from some sort of severance agreement for him to set up his own company, D. Drummond & Son, which kept him occupied for some four years. The core products of this small concern, in the early days, were mainly industrial locomotives and railcars. One example of the former consisted of some seven narrow gauge engines for the Glasgow Corporation's gasworks at Dawsholm. Of 0-4-0WT layout, Nos. 9-15 were of 2 ft gauge and served there for many years, the last example not being scrapped until March 1957. Clearly, the narrow gauge exercise for Glasgow Corporation put the company on the map for such locomotives, for there were sundry other examples for enterprises elsewhere, one being for a batch of ten 4-4-0s for the Beira-Umtali line in Mozambique and Rhodesia. These locomotives were built to drawings furnished by George Pauling, builder of that line, produced by his Works Manager A. Lawley. They eventually became known as 'Lawleys'. Owing to the gauge restriction, outside cylinders had to be employed. The resulting locomotive carried no Drummond features and one of the total of 42 eventually supplied (the other 32 coming from the Brush Electrical Engineering, which had just been formed from the Falcon Engine and Car Co.) still exists in South Africa, preserved in working order on the Sandstone Heritage Trust narrow gauge line south of Johannesburg near the Lesotho border. This does not appear to be one produced by D. Drummond & Son, but serves as a good example of the type produced.

There were also sundry odd examples for collieries and factories elsewhere. Some of the railcars were, surprisingly, for New South Wales, so clearly, some good had come from his Australian jaunt. This form of transport was to reappear later during his days on the London & South Western Railway.

However, by 1895, opportunity beckoned back in England, when the post of Locomotive Superintendent of the LSWR became advertised following the announcement of the retirement of William Adams, the current holder of that post. Adams was 71 and his mental health had been giving cause for concern for some time, as what we now know as senile dementure crept upon him, and he was gently persuaded to retire by a concerned Board of Directors. A new man was needed in the minimum of time, and Dugald could offer the necessary expertise, was available at short notice, and his locomotive designs on the NBR and CR were proof of sound engineering practice. He applied for the post, and got it. Handing over control of his small company to his sons Walter and George, he prepared to invade the LSWR works at Nine Elms. His two sons were vested as partners in the concern and continued to run it in the absence of their father. It was eventually absorbed with the nearby Glasgow Railway Company to form the Glasgow Railway Engineering Co. Ltd in 1901.

This small engineering company thus formed in Glasgow continued for quite a few years after Dugald had departed Scotland for what was to be the final time, existing largely on small sub-contracts for the railway industry in Britain and overseas, eventually involved mainly in the production of wheels, tyres, axles and springs. Obviously the success of this business was reasonable enough, for in the early years of the 1900s a controlling interest was bought by Sir James Lithgow, in order to provide yet another outlet for what was to become a great engineering and shipbuilding enterprise. The exact date of this take-over is not known, but the fact that Walter died in 1905, leaving George in overall control suggests that it could have been after Dugald's death. George would then have no one to fall back onto for advice and support, Peter not being on record as having any interest in that enterprise. In the mid-1930s it then became a subsidiary of Beardmore's making the same products and was finally wound up in 1958 at the time when Beardmore's was gradually running down to closure.

When Dugald's appointment on the LSWR became known to the ARLE, he was soon invited to rejoin their ranks. He was recorded as being present at the November 1895 meeting, at the St Pancras Hotel, and was immediately selected as Vice-President for the following year. The Secretary at that time was James Stirling, Locomotive Superintendent of the South Eastern Railway, who had the sad news of the death of his brother Patrick, Locomotive Superintendent of the Great Northern Railway, to report. The business of the meeting covered the running of short wheelbase locomotives at speed over main lines, tyre thicknesses for express engines, rail sections and spacings of check-rails. No significant contributions were recorded from Dugald. He was, however, back in the thick of the railway engineering scene in Britain and was to make a significant contribution to a major English railway over the next 17 years.

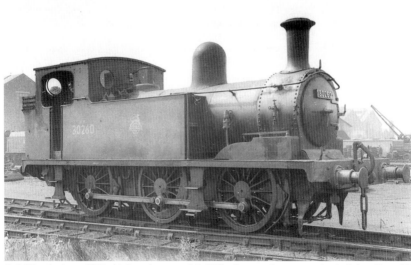

0-6-0T of class 'G6' (Adams) a useful little locomotive perpetuated by Dugald Drummond; Eastleigh 24th May, 1956, approaching 60 years of age.   *R.G. Jarvis/MRT*

Chapter Six

The Early Days at Nine Elms

William Adams, the Locomotive Superintendent of the LSWR was as much an artist as an engineer. Although trained as a marine engineer he had switched to the railway scene early on in his career, coming to the LSWR in 1878 via the North London and Great Eastern railways. His locomotives were examples of meticulous Victorian workmanship, sturdily built, and good performers. He had, like so many others of his time, also made sure that parts were interchangeable between specific classes. On the personality side, Adams was a large, cheery, bearded man with many talents other than his obvious engineering skills. He sang, enjoyed entertaining and as his large family increased in size and moved away to follow their own lives (he had 10 children) they could be found visiting him at home in the large Victorian edifice, Carlton House, on Putney Hill. At work, his easy-going demeanour made him popular with the employees and rarely did he have to exert much pressure on them to get what he wanted. Offenders were dealt with face to face in a calm manner and the message that any further trouble would result in dismissal imparted. Nine Elms was a relaxed and happy place to be working, if a little lax in efficiency.

As he approached his seventies, his life, up to then lived with great zest, took a turn for the worse. He appeared to be getting vague in some statements and the old sharp zeal appeared to be slipping away. He would also suddenly lose track of what he was saying in mid-sentence. More and more the Works Manager, W.F. Pettigrew, had to organize his own day around Adams vagueness to keep matters running smoothly. The LSWR Directors, once alerted to the problem, realised that things could not go on like this and moves were made to induce Adams' retirement and appoint a successor.

The Great Western Railway was, in a few years, to go through a similar episode with William Dean, its Locomotive Superintendent, as a gradual and stealthy loss of memory affected that worthy engineer. That concern was lucky enough to have an extremely capable successor in George Churchward, who was gradually eased into place at the end of the century. The LSWR Directors appeared to pass over Pettigrew, who was a very competent Works Manager and excellent engineer, preferring to search elsewhere for a dynamic new Locomotive Superintendent.

Accordingly, in 1895, Adams accepted retirement at the age of 71. He lived on quietly in No. 7 Amersham Road, a substantial house in Putney, until he was eighty, a pleasantly smiling, strangely silent, giant of a man. His wife had died some time previously, a fact which could not have helped his condition. For company he had his widowed daughter Isabella and her daughter Nancy. They were attended by a retinue of four staff. Railway developments and political events passed him by as he spent his final years in his own thoughts, occasionally bursting into song. Old Daddy Adams, as he was known to the locals, died in 1904.

To replace William Adams came Dugald Drummond, plucked from his small company in Glasgow. The starting salary was £1,500, considerably less than he had been getting on the CR in 1890, but the Board of the LSWR were always looking for a bargain. His reputation gained on his successive posts on the NBR and CR had much to do with his appointment on the LSWR. Nine Elms was about to receive a great jolt when Dugald took office. No more the casual approach of Adams, but a fierce inroad into work practices, discipline and works reorganization was to come. Drummond took up the reins of office with vigour and started making changes immediately. Should any oppose him, there was a strong hint of resignation flung in their direction. Should that fail to curb their misplaced zeal, dismissal lurked around the corner. Many heads rolled as Dugald exercised his authority, being replaced in some instances by an inroad of eager Scotsmen well versed in fulfilling his commands.

One such import was Robert Wallace Urie, to replace W.F. Pettigrew as Works Manager. The opportunity to take the Locomotive Superintendency of the Furness Railway had fortuitously come along for Pettigrew, who quite probably was smarting from the passing over of what should have been a normal progression to the LSWR Superintendency. He also was probably keen to get away from the blunt criticism and outspoken comments of Drummond. The change from Adams' polite calm orders to Dugald's rough and direct demands requiring immediate action was clearly too much for some to absorb.

Urie had become Dugald's chief draughtsman at St Rollox and, since 1891, had been Works Manager there. Another opposite in manner and temperament, his acceptance as a trusted aide had been cemented by a row at St Rollox, as recounted by J.C. Urie, Robert's son:

> Many years ago, at St Rollox, Drummond had an argument with my father and left the office in a bad humour. My father discovered later that they had both been wrong, and went to Drummond's office and told him so. Drummond growled at him, and told him to get out of his office, but from that day they never had any further hard words.

Shortly after taking office Dugald instigated weekly progress meetings at which schedules for locomotives undergoing or awaiting repair were agreed. Also, on Monday mornings there were meetings in Dugald's office to cover the previous week's mishaps reported to him in connection with the handling of trains. To be summoned to one of these latter meetings invariably meant that the culprit needed to have a good explanation ready to offer in the grilling he was to receive. New construction, dependent upon the supply of parts was also covered and provisional dates for completion fixed. The insistence that these programmes had to be adhered to resulted in some months of chaos at Nine Elms. However, the able efforts of Robert Urie ensured that, eventually, order was restored and resulted not only in the schedules being met, but bettered in that general repairs now took some five working days less to complete. By the autumn of 1896, Nine Elms was operating at maximum efficiency and many of the employees had altered their opinion of Dugald. He had played his hand forcefully and was now accepted.

As with many Locomotive Superintendents of the day, Dugald not only held sway over the design, construction and servicing of the locomotive stock, he also covered the engine crews and shed staff. One particular fact upon which he came down hard almost immediately after taking office, was drinking on duty.

As soon as his enquiries into such matters had sought out those reported as slipping into a station refreshment room for a quick pint, and especially anything stronger, when in charge of a locomotive, they were immediately dismissed. Although those delegated to report the miscreants dutifully made known their task to those they were watching when they began their watch, so those enginemen who flagrantly took no notice of this warning paid the price for their actions.

As his position became established on the LSWR, he would be found briefing the drivers of key expresses, exhorting them to keep time so far as weather conditions and speed restrictions would permit.

Not only was the time keeping insisted upon, but driving techniques often were an important subject upon which Dugald would take issue with his enginemen. A very competent driver himself, he set to and wrote a handbook: *Lectures Delivered to Enginemen and Firemen of the L&SWR on the Management of Their Engines* which was made available to all LSWR drivers as a guide for their handling of locomotives. As regards how his locomotives were to be treated, he issued strict orders against 'thrashing' them. If he had knowledge of this occurring the driver concerned would most certainly be 'carpeted', for a hard used engine suffered greater than average wear which increased maintenance costs. To further encourage economic running he had introduced a coal bonus scheme for all engine crews.

In spite of his aggressive behaviour, Dugald soon acquired a following from his staff and enginemen. He was, they discovered, one of those managers who believed in being in touch personally with them. Despite his fearsome reputation he was approachable to deliver judgements on matters relevant to the construction, maintenance or handling of his locomotives, though they had to have a cast-iron case to place before him.

So far as production matters were concerned, Dugald had found the works busy on the construction of Adams' last designs. A batch of ten 'O2' 0-4-4Ts, four 'T6' 4-4-0s and four 'X6' 4-4-0s were outshopped in 1896. He also kept the 'G6' 0-6-0T in production until 1900, so useful were these little goods tanks.

Walter and George had by now both settled into an engineering career and were still running the small company set up by Dugald after his return from Australia. Walter's contacts with outside contractors led him into the company of the daughter of one of them, one Elizabeth Harkness Wall. Her father, John Wall, had died prior to 1896 and she and her sister Isabella lived with their widowed mother at an imposing house, The Acre in Maryhill.

By now the small works was keeping the brothers reasonably well occupied, interspersed with occasional visits to their father in London for advice and support. Walter proposed to Elizabeth Wall, was accepted and a date for the wedding was soon set. So, on 3rd December, 1896 the marriage took place in Maryhill at The Acre. It would have been an event tinged with sadness, for Dugald and Peter's father had died, in Ardrossan, earlier that year at the age of 80. However, it would have been a grand get-together for the Drummond family, with Dugald and Peter from their respective Locomotive Superintendencies sharing reminiscences from times past and looking ahead to their futures.

The Adams 'T3' express 4-4-0 in full Drummond lining. Very free steamers, these were popular with the crews. No. 563 was built in 1893 and proved to be the last of the class to be withdrawn in 1945. *John Scott-Morgan Collection*

This Adams 'T6' was built as Dugald Drummond took office. A graceful locomotive in full Drummond lining; 7th August, 1902. *R.K. Blencowe/John Scott-Morgan Collection*

Having asserted his authority and begun to instil a rigid level of discipline amongst his men, Dugald turned his mind to the supply of new locomotives. The first design to appear was the 'M7' 0-4-4T, based on his earlier NBR class '157', but larger. In fact the 'M7' was to be the largest and most powerful of this type ever built. Its tractive effort of 19,750 lb. made it a versatile machine to be found on a wide range of tasks over the system. In all 105 were to be constructed, all at Nine Elms save for the final 10 at Eastleigh in 1911. There was also a strong link to the Stroudley 'D' class 0-4-2T, the 'M7' being described by some as a lengthened version of that popular Brighton design, with the rear carrying wheels replaced by a bogie.

Concurrent with the 'M7', a goods 0-6-0 design appeared, based on his earlier NBR and CR 0-6-0s. The requirement for this design came from an earlier request to Adams for additional 0-6-0s, which had been put off due to his encroaching illness. The boiler, cylinders and motion of the Drummond offering were interchangeable with those of the 'M7'. As space at Nine Elms was limited, the order for the thirty '700' class went to Dübs in Glasgow. Co-incidentally, as Dübs were turning out the LSWR 0-6-0s, they were also engaged in quoting for a batch of 0-6-0s of Peter Drummond's design for the HR. When the relative dimensions and weights of the two 0-6-0s are compared it is patently obvious that Dugald had given Peter a set of drawings to work on.

With these two initial designs, Dugald had set his stamp on the future LSWR locomotive designs to flow from his fertile mind.

Having fulfilled the needs for general duties and freight work, the matter of the express fleet needs raised its head. Drummond's first essay into this sphere, in 1897, seemed a hotchpotch of sundry ideas he had collected together over the years. The genesis of the 'T7', or 'Double-Single' as it was better known, came about as follows.

Single-drivers were enjoying an Indian Summer of use for express purposes, their free-running characteristics offering excellent performance and the lack of motion for coupled wheels giving low maintenance costs. On the MR Johnson had turned out over 100 examples of his Single designs, the GNR Stirling Singles were turning in some creditable performances and Dean on the GWR had produced a range of 2-2-2s and 4-2-2s, amongst many more. This proliferation of such locomotives had been brought about by two factors; firstly the low train weights prevalent and secondly, the advent of steam sanding gear to prevent excessive slipping, always the bane of drivers when adhesion was via a single pair of wheels. The LSWR Directors had noted all these developments on the other railways and had pressured Adams to consider a single-wheeler design. Some schemes had been turned out by the drawing office but were sidelined when Dugald arrived. The Board continued to push for such a locomotive and it was the 'Double-Single' that was offered to satisfy their request. On this basis it is not difficult to see the agreement to release funding for Dugald's proposal. What had been overlooked by the Board was the steady increase in train weights as demand for traffic grew. Dugald recognised this and therefore came up with his answer to the Directors' demands and the train loading trend.

The class 'T7' single example initially produced was, at first sight, a four-cylinder 4-4-0, but on a closer inspection the driving wheels were seen not to be

'M7' class 0-4-4T No. 44, a Nine Elms product of 1899, on a passenger duty.

John Scott-Morgan Collection

'M7' No. 243, built Nine Elms 1897, complete with conical smoke box door; Nine Elms *c.*1901.

John Scott-Morgan Collection

The single example of the 'M7', No. 726, which was superheated by Urie, seen in 1922.
John Scott-Morgan Collection

'M7' No. 28 on a local passenger turn in SR days.   *John Scott-Morgan Collection*

'M7' No. 30038 in malachite livery at Eastleigh 5th September, 1948.
John Scott-Morgan Collection

'M7' No. 30053, now preserved on the Swanage Railway, in its final years on BR, shunting at Brighton station.   *R.G. Jarvis/MRT*

'700' class 0-6-0 No. 696. *John Scott-Morgan Collection*

'700' class 0-6-0 No. 692 in as-built condition with conical smokebox door, has a goods train in tow on a tender-first run. *John Scott-Morgan Collection*

The prototype double-single, No. 720 (class 'T7') approaches Wimbledon on an express duty. This has the larger boiler which dates the photograph to 1905 or after.

John Scott-Morgan Collection

The prototype double-single No. 720 after re-boilering.   *John Scott-Morgan Collection*

coupled together, the front pair driven by the inside cylinders and the rear pair driven by the outside cylinders, making it a 4-2-2-0. To further complicate things the valve gear was dissimilar, Stephenson's for the inside motion and Joys for the outside. The free running characteristics of the single driver was clearly one of the aims of this design, but some disadvantages showed immediately, for, should one set of driving wheels slip, even momentarily, the beat would get all out of tune. The resulting effect on the draughting could be detrimental to say the least. Grossly over-cylindered, the original boiler proved inadequate and the cylinders as built, of 16½ inch diameter were progressively lined up to 14 inches. Even then a larger boiler had, eventually, to be provided, such was the demand for steam from the reduced size. *Appendix Seven* gives a brief appraisal of some aspects of the design philosophy leading to this unorthodox locomotive.

Quite probably, it seems that Dugald could have been influenced on this design to some considerable degree by F.W. Webb's 2-2-2-0 compound developments on the LNWR which employed uncoupled driving wheels. Now, the latest of these compounds, the 'Teutonics', were getting a reputation for fast, free, running and, whilst not being particularly keen on adopting compounding himself, Drummond did follow the uncoupled concept. After all, the locomotive was intended for express work and free running was a key requirement. Additionally, the outside Joy's valve gear was a definite copy of the Webb layout.

Another Drummond innovation appeared on this 'Double-Single', this being the firebox cross water tubes, which increased the heating surface at the point of greatest heat concentration. Dugald also claimed that the circulation around the firebox was improved as well with the cross tubes acting as a form of spark arrester. Interestingly, this first version was produced without the external access covers so common to other Drummond designs employing such fireboxes, although, when re-boilered later they did appear. Successive iterations were made to try and improve an indifferent performer, the most bizarre being the installation of steam sanding gear discharging onto the rails between the bogie wheels! Such was Dugald's overbearing attitude it appears that no one could summon up the courage to query this strange modification for some time.

The 'Double-Single' was, in fact, one of the first four-cylinder types built in Britain. It being beaten, by a few weeks, by firstly the No. 11 4-4-0 of James Manson on the G&SWR and, secondly, Frank Webb's experimental 4-4-0 built for comparison with his 4-cylinder compound 4-4-0 on the LNWR. The four-cylinder layout was to come into play on many railways in the 20th century, particularly for express locomotives, despite the increased complexity of the motion and extra maintenance that produced. So, at least the basic concept was of the very latest design thinking.

The odd driver could handle the 4-2-2-0 and one in particular, driver Geary of Nine Elms, produced some impressive runs once the reboilering had taken place. However, there are no surviving records remaining to give an idea as to the performance attained.

The 'T7' also introduced the Drummond double-bogie tender, or 'watercart', to the scene. This was to be found on many of his future designs and was

'E10' class 'Double-Single' No. 373 has a substantial express, plus steam to spare. Approaching Surbiton certainly after 1916. *John Scott-Morgan Collection*

'Double-Single' No. 371, class 'E10', has an easy task with just four coaches on a stopping service.

instantly recognisable by the inside bearings to the bogie wheels. This was due to Dugald's inbuilt sense of economy, for the wheels were the same as those employed on the leading bogies of his 4-4-0s and 4-6-0s. To simplify construction of the tender, they were made frameless with the bogie centre supports riveted directly onto the tender well. A short while after entering service some loosening of the attachments began and water seeped out onto the track. This led to the nickname of 'watercarts' after the old horse-drawn vehicles which sprayed the roads to keep the dust down in hot, dry, weather.

With the advent of the 'M7' and '700' classes in substantial numbers, it appears that the LSWR Board did not worry too much about the above excursion into a radical new approach to express motive power. The existing Adams' designs, then employed on such tasks, being reliable free-running engines, were capable of meeting the demands of express work at that time. The prototype 'Double-Single' soldiered on, being joined by a batch of five slightly altered variants in 1901, class 'E10'. These unusual locomotives lived on into Southern days, being little used and very unpopular with the enginemen, until Maunsell condemned them to the scrap line in 1926-7. The big mystery surrounding the 'Double-Singles' was the building of this latter batch of clearly troublesome and inadequate locomotives. The Drummond stubbornness had showed through here in its extreme and was to reappear later, in some features, with the advent of the first LSWR 4-6-0s as we shall see later.

The first real move towards a normal 4-4-0 appeared in 1898. Ten examples of the 'C8' class, based on Dugald's NBR '476' and CR '66' classes, being built. These never very useful locomotives were intended for semi-fast work but proved indifferent steamers due to a smallish firebox, quickly being relegated to secondary duties after a few months of struggling on the relatively heavy Bournemouth and Salisbury expresses. It was as though Dugald was feeling his way on the LSWR, for his caution extended to keeping this first 4-4-0 offering free of the gadgetry to plague many of his later designs, with only a steam reverser, located rather inaccessibly between the frames, to worry the maintenance staff.

The steam reverser had been incorporated to ease the driver's workload. Dugald was quite experienced as a driver and knew first-hand of the hard effort needed for lever reverse, particularly when constantly shifting gear to effect a new cut-off position. Another steam reverser advocate, Wainwright of the South Eastern & Chatham Railway (SECR), did at least mount his equipment on the running plate where it was accessible for servicing.

After taking in the disappointing steaming performance of the 'C8', Dugald made sure that all future designs had a more substantial grate area. This was one underlying reason for his later 4-4-0 locomotives excellent steaming capabilities. Grate area was, according to Chapelon in later years, of greater importance than the absolute heating surface.

It was also in 1898 that Walter and Elizabeth became the proud parents of a daughter, Elizabeth, at their home, No. 22, Newton Place in Glasgow.

In this year an 'M7' had a minor mishap. One of the early duties on which this class of tank was used involved that of coping with some express passenger trains between Exeter and Plymouth. This was a difficult route and on 6th

'C8' No. 773, is rostered for a special taking Lord Kitchener from Southampton to London, 12th February, 1902. The gentlemen are: *left to right*, inspector Wilkinson, inspector Moore and driver James, the latter being the selected driver for 'The Bug'.

R.K. Blencowe/J. Scott-Morgan Collection

A 'C8' 4-4-0, number indecipherable, when fitted with the 8-wheel 'watercart' tender *c*.1903.

John Scott-Morgan Collection

March No. 252 left the track on a curve near Tavistock. The resulting pile-up was, thankfully only to produce injuries to some passengers and at the following inquiry the inspector criticised both the locomotive and the condition of the track. Dugald's comments on the former are not on record but the 'M7s' were withdrawn from this area and put onto suburban work around London.

Whilst on the Scottish railways Dugald had, gradually, over the years, discarded many of the Stroudley-inspired fads connected with feed water, he took the opportunity to reintroduce his own versions of these on the LSWR. Some years before, in Joseph Beattie's days there had been a considerable amount of experimentation with feed-water heating devices so Dugald had little opposition from the Locomotive Committee in implementing his own similar systems. These were to plague LSWR crews for many years to come.

The company house provided by the LSWR in 1902 for Dugald and his family was in South Bank, Surbiton and at some time after this it was renamed 'Morven' by Dugald. The name chosen was that of a notable peak in the Eastern Highlands which was visible from the HR main line to Thurso and Wick. This sizeable property overlooked Surbiton station and the main line on the up side. Before this his home, in the 1901 Census return, is listed as 'South Bank Lodge'. (A nearby neighbour to this property was Archibald Scott, since 1884 a Director of the LSWR. Scott had been General Manager of the line since 1852 and was largely responsible for the leasing agreement with the MR for the Somerset & Dorset Railway.) A cook, parlour-maid and housemaid comprised the staff required to keep affairs in order for the family.

This home, a stone's throw from the station, was also very convenient for boarding 'The Bug' for the journey to work when that mode of transport emerged in 1899. It also gave Dugald the opportunity to go down to the station at any time he was at home, and watch his enginemen and their charges in operation. Should anything seem amiss in the condition or handling of a locomotive, startled passengers awaiting their train were jerked into awareness of the presence of authority by a strident Scottish voice shouting blunt comments above the noise of the passing train.

By 1901, there was only the next to youngest daughter Janet left permanently at home with her parents. Walter and George were still up in Glasgow, and the little engineering business, according to available information, continued to pay its way with small sub-contracts for the railway industry especially now it had been merged with the nearby Glasgow Railway Company. Up to then it appears that they often came down to visit and keep their father up-to-date on the state of the business. They clearly still relied on his advice and assistance.

'The Bug' at Eastleigh, *c.*1910.   *John Scott-Morgan Collection*

'The Bug' in pristine condition, stands ready for service.   *John Scott-Morgan Collection*

Chapter Seven

Personal Transport and
Further 4-4-0 Developments

Drummond's success with his locomotives on the Scottish railways was due largely to the free-steaming boilers which had adequate grate area to permit almost unlimited steam generation. Also, we have seen his subtle improvements to the cylinders and valves ensured that this steam could be used expansively to good effect thus ensuring good economy of fuel and water consumption. Additionally his designs were noted for their free-running characteristics.

As train weights increased and the track was improved to take greater axle loads it was possible to make considerable increases in boiler size and weight. This ensured that the 4-4-0 could grow and thus produce the power needed to deal with the heavier trains. The CR 4-4-0 developments after Dugald had left were all enlarged versions of those introduced by him, resulting in one of the best families of express 4-4-0s to be found on the Scottish pre-Grouping lines. So, it was not surprising that his 4-4-0 developments for the LSWR stemmed directly from those he had concluded with on the CR, as we shall see. There were a string of other developments of that classic wheel arrangement to come, but before launching into the story of what happened, a short diversion into the saga of 'Mr Drummond's Car', as it was portrayed to the LSWR Board, is appropriate.

As the turn of the new century approached, Dugald spent considerable time travelling the railway keeping a check on his crews. Also, by now he was beginning to formulate plans to provide new locomotive building facilities and the site for this was to be at Eastleigh, where the LSWR carriage works were already sited. There was adequate spare land available for purchase close to the carriage works.

Dugald, realising that when this development took place he would be involved in much travelling between London and Eastleigh, asked the Board for funds to permit the construction of a small personal saloon for this. As the Board was, by now, well satisfied with his production of new locomotives, to save any argument with their irascible, but highly competent, Locomotive Superintendent, they agreed to this request. So, in 1899, there appeared what became known as 'The Bug', a small 4-2-4T which incorporated, at the rear, a small saloon which contained some chairs, a small buffet, a toilet and, most important of all, a sliding flap opening into the cab.

It is wondered if the genesis of 'The Bug' sprang from a LB&SCR 2-4-2T with a rear saloon built by Stroudley in 1889 for that line's Civil Engineer for inspecting track, bridges, tunnels, etc. Originally this had been a Sharp, Stewart 2-4-0T of 1869 used on the Hayling Island branch until displaced by a 'Terrier'. As No. 481, given the name *Inspector* it served in its intended capacity until withdrawal in 1899.

Dugald used his little locomotive for getting to and from work and in his tours of inspection. Often a crew could be pleasantly trundling down the four track main line to Basingstoke only to be jerked into sudden awareness that their performance was being watched, with the arrival of the 'Bug' alongside. Should excessive smoke be evident, or the engine look at all unkempt, the 'Bug's' droplight would be lowered and a blast of invective would ring across the gap. Invariably, the next day would come a summons to the office at Nine Elms for explanation of the misdemeanour. Enginemen very quickly became aware of the need to adhere strictly to the rules that governed their actions and the locomotive's performance.

The crew of the 'Bug' were hand-picked by Dugald and for many years faithfully served their master, learning to react to his whims at all times. As for other crews, if the 'Bug' was not visible, they often found that, during a station stop, they were liable to have an unannounced visitor join them on the footplate. Dugald was also known to have ordered drivers to stand aside for him to take over and demonstrate the driving technique he preferred. Sometimes this would completely unnerve the fireman and, if pressure started to drop, sparks would fly in his direction. Dugald was absolutely scathing over any minor misdemeanour and it took a stout heart to withstand his commands without them having an effect upon performance. Sometimes the driver might be an old stager like the one who, seeing Drummond's presence completely fluster his young fireman, had the presence of mind to say firmly: 'The lad's all right, sir, if you'll only let him alone!' Straightforward approaches like that were quietly appreciated by Dugald and he would simmer down.

One fact about the use of 'The Bug' was Dugald's complete ignoring of the upset to traffic timing caused by its sudden appearances, more particularly when he was engaged in one of his sudden inspection jaunts. One often wonders how many times delays were caused leading to frustrated passengers missing a vital connection. Such events were totally brushed aside and quite probably the LSWR Traffic Department had to fend off or placate complaining passengers. However, the LSWR was quite adept at juggling the paths after many years of fitting in specials for the military and shipping companies, sometimes at very short notice, so complaints were probably minimised.

For his crew of this personal transport Dugald chose carefully. He needed men who were willing to work under his close supervision, were utterly reliable and clearly willing to be on call at very short notice all the time. The driver, James, who filled this bill for many years was teamed up with a William Eaton as fireman and this crew kept him happy with their handling of the 'Bug'.

There were times when the hatchway to the cab was much in use on their journeying. Should progress appear to be slow an appropriate rejoinder would sound through, a typical example being: 'What's the matter, James, d'ye think this is a goods train?'

Eaton's fire would also be inspected before some journeys, for Dugald was meticulous about correct firing techniques. He had been known to order a crew of a delayed train off their footplate and take Eaton with him as fireman to run that train on to its destination, with the deposed enginemen following on somewhat miserably for the inevitable carpeting.

Drummond's forays to the extremities of the LSWR system were legendary. He was liable to appear without any forewarning at the most out-of-the-way engine shed. A classic example of this form of visitation was a trip down the

North Cornwall line, a long journey for the 'Bug', this being the furthest West one could travel on the LSWR. The return journey was hampered by being put in a path behind a particularly slow goods train, and Drummond decided to stay overnight at Exeter. The 'Bug' was halted at Ashbury in order to telegraph ahead for accommodation, but this was not immediately possible as the persons employed there who had the training to operate the telegraph instruments were, by this time (it was well past seven o'clock in the evening), off duty and firmly settled at a Hunt Supper evening!

On learning this, Dugald began to make his feelings felt on the lack of anyone competent around and clearly this was overheard by Eaton, his fireman, who had, in the past, spent some time in the Traffic Department and knew how to operate the telegraph. He offered to try his hand and succeeded in getting a suitable message to Exeter, for which he got a comment from a mollified Drummond of: 'You're not such a fool as you look, Eaton!'

The 'Bug' was easily identified by its disc headcode setting, the same as for that used on the Royal train. The only difference was that Drummond specified the white discs to have red edging, compared to the plain white of that for the Royal train. At night it must have been quite confusing when lights were substituted!

The second Drummond 4-4-0 to grace LSWR metals was to become a classic. This was the 'T9', or 'Greyhound' as it became popularly known. Excellent performers from the start, 66 were built between 1899 and 1901. Sturdily constructed, they were all to have a long life of 50 years or more, being superheated by Urie and Maunsell between 1922 and 1924, a move which transformed their already excellent performance into an outstanding one for their size. One example, thankfully, has been preserved and is now part of the National Collection at the National Railway Museum (NRM).

Try as he may, Dugald could never get the agreement of the Board to allow the naming of locomotives. It has been said that as the LB&SCR indulged in that practice, the LSWR would never follow suit. However, the Brighton named many of its locomotives after places served by that railway, which occasionally led to confusion amongst passengers, some of whom thought the name on the engine referred to the ultimate destination of the train it was hauling!

Despite the cramped conditions at Nine Elms works, Dugald's reorganization of the shops wrought such an improvement in working practices that the production costs of the 'T9' were amongst the lowest in Britain. Likewise, the repair costs were held down to around a total of £700 over a five-year period if no boiler change was involved; £140 per year per engine was economic indeed.

Following the 'T9' came two batches of mixed traffic 4-4-0s, the 'K10' and 'L11'. These designs differed only in the coupled wheelbase, 9 ft for the 'K10' and 10 ft for the 'L11', and the firebox lengths. Forty of each type were built, the 'K10s' in 1901-2 and the 'L11' between 1903 and 1907. The 'K10' also came with six-wheeled tenders, whereas the 'L11' had eight-wheeled 4,000 gallon 'water carts' built for them, but only nine of them actually received them, the remainder being swapped with the six-wheeled units from the 'C8' and 'T9' classes.

Fully aware of the need to have a good grate area after the indifferent steaming of the 'C8s', Dugald specified a 10 ft coupled wheelbase of all his

'T9' class 4-4-0 No. 712, of the first 1899 Dübs batch displays the neat lining-out specified by Dugald Drummond.   *John Scott-Morgan Collection*

This sharp photograph of 'T9' No. 728 shows the Drummond lining clearly.
John Scott-Morgan Collection

'T9' No. 337 has been fitted with a Westinghouse pump and would have been employed on air-braked stock workings. *John Scott-Morgan Collection*

'T9' class No. 117, built at Nine Elms in 1899, awaits departure from Waterloo *c.*1912. *John Scott-Morgan Collection*

Meldon viaduct, now a listed structure, provides a good vantage point to photograph this 'T9'. Although in LSWR livery, this was taken in SR days on 14th July, 1924.

John Scott-Morgan Collection

No. 314, a 'T9' built at Nine Elms in 1901 with 6-wheel tender, passes through Clapham Junction under the ex-LB&SCR overhead wires, shortly to be removed, 9th April, 1928.

John Scott-Morgan Collection

'T9' No. 30313 in later superheated condition and with 6-wheel tender, built at Nine Elms in 1901, is seen at Eastleigh shed, 14th July, 1950.   *J.M. Jarvis*

No. 342, a 'K10' 4-4-0 (Nine Elms 1901) in original condition at Weymouth. Forty of these mixed traffic designs were built and acquired the nickname 'Small Hoppers'.

John Scott-Morgan Collection

A Urie firebox water tube removal exercise was carried out on 'K10' class 4-4-0 No. 140. She is seen resting between turns *c*.1920. *John Scott-Morgan Collection*

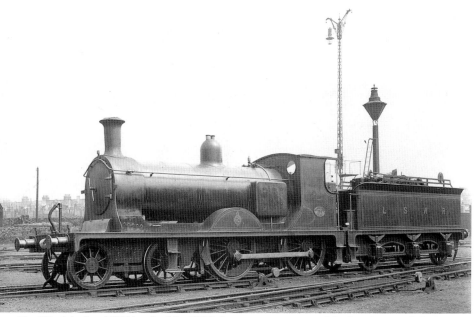

No. 391 of the last (1902) batch of the 'K10' class.   *John Scott-Morgan Collection*

The first of the 40-strong 'L11' class 4-4-0s, or 'Large Hopper', built at Nine Elms in 1903, on shed at Nine Elms *c*.1920.   *John Scott-Morgan Collection*

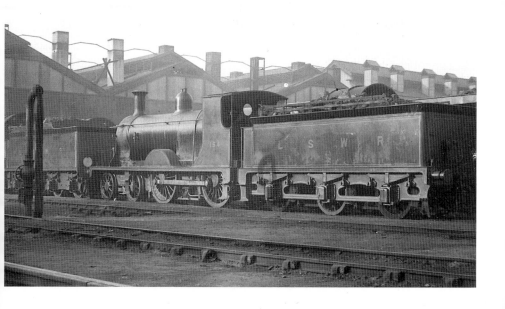

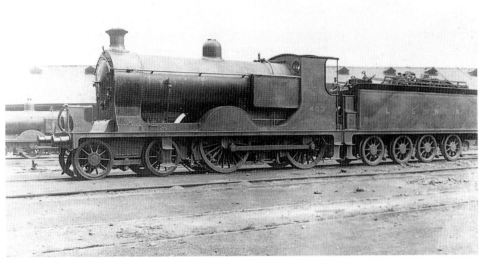

'S11' class 4-4-0 No. 403 in as-built condition at Nine Elms shed, 12th June, 1920.

John Scott-Morgan Collection

'S11' No. 397 departs Waterloo on an express duty *c*.1910.   *John Scott-Morgan Collection*

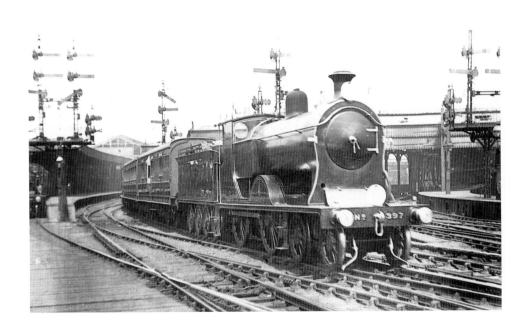

future 4-4-0s, apart from the 'K10s'. This permitted a 7 ft 4 in.-long firebox giving a grate area of 24 sq. ft. This 10 ft length of coupling rods was considered by some as risky, but no bending at high speeds took place. The rods were of flat rectangular cross-section as adopted by Churchward of the GWR on the majority of his locomotives from about this time.

Some experimental work on boilers extended from the early cross tubes in the firebox, which in themselves gave quite good results. This encouraged some studies into a radical new layout incorporating a single central flue which had no fewer than 215 water tubes across its length at a range of angles. This large flue was augmented by 18 conventional fire tubes. With a total heating surface of 737 sq. ft this boiler proved a good steamer, perhaps slightly better than a conventional one, despite the somewhat reduced heating surface when compared to the 1,292 sq. ft of the conventional unit. However, its complicated construction was a continual source of trouble. Only one was ever built and was fitted to 'K10' No. 343 until changed for a normal unit in 1906.

The batches of the class 'L11' built in 1906-7 incorporated duplex feed pumps instead of the injectors originally fitted to the earlier batches. These fittings were expensive and had a distinctive sound when operating. On later express locomotives they were frequently heard running and, with the automatic cylinder safety valves used to ease any cylinder compression when drifting, a locomotive running into a station sounded more like a marine engine than a railway engine.

For the ARLE summer meeting in 1902 Dugald arranged to host this on behalf of the LSWR at the Crown Hotel, Lyndhurst, to which venue the members were conveyed in a specially appointed carriage, attached to a regular train, down the main line from Waterloo. The main subject for discussion was that of standard specifications for materials used in the construction of locomotives and rolling stock. G.J. Churchward, a new member attending for the first time in place of William Dean, was immediately given the job of co-ordinating the views of all ARLE members on this particular matter.

Before his 4-6-0s appeared, Dugald brought out two more classes of 4-4-0s. The first to appear, the 'S11', was basically the 'L11' with 6 ft coupled wheels and a bigger boiler. Firebox water tubes and a watercart tender were standard. Ten were built in 1903, all at Nine Elms. It was on this class that Drummond introduced his built-up crank axle which became a standard feature on all future locomotives. Made up of nine parts, the webs of the crank arms were designed to avoid the use of balance weights in the wheels, and the design was patented. The constituent parts were assembled by shrinkage in preference to forcing together by hydraulic pressure, the shrinkage allowance being 0.0029 inches per inch of diameter. Suitable precautions were provided to prevent any shifting in the remote possibility of a hot box occurring.

Another Drummond simple, but effective, feature involved the regulator spindle in the backhead. This was tapered down from the inside and held in place mainly by boiler pressure, which effectively prevented leakage into the cab environment. As regards design details or improvements to his locomotives, Dugald was fiercely opposed to any which came from elsewhere. This can be illustrated by the following episode in which a driver came to see

'S11' No. 395, the first of the class, at Waterloo in 1910. A handsome engine indeed.

John Scott-Morgan Collection

'S11' No. 30397 had, by BR days, acquired a 6-wheel tender and a rather squat stove-pipe chimney: Fratton shed 14th July, 1950. *J.M. Jarvis*

him with a suggestion for a minor improvement. Dugald listened carefully, then got up from his desk and motioned the driver to sit at it. The driver refused, somehow sensing the oncoming blast: 'And why dinna ye like it? Because ye know it's my bloody job to build the engines and yours to drive them'.

Following the 'S11' came the 'L12', which was merely the former with 6 ft 7 in. coupled wheels. A total of 20 appeared from Nine Elms in 1904. No. 421 of this batch was involved in a major accident at Salisbury in 1906. As it approached Salisbury, hauling the special boat express from Devonport, it was observed to be travelling at high speed and the whistle was blowing continuously. Clearly something was amiss and the driver was giving some warning of problems. The signalman at Salisbury West Box estimated the speed to be at least 60 mph, probably more, as it passed him. The train was a light one, consisting of a brake van, three first class saloons and a kitchen brake car. There were 43 passengers on board who had arrived at Devonport on the American Line's *New York*.

At the east end of Salisbury station, on the up side, was a sharp curve with a speed limit of 30 mph. In the Bournemouth bay stood an 0-6-0 No. 0351, and between this and the up fast road a milk empties train was drifting into the station. As No. 421 entered the sharp curve at its excessive speed, it tilted over far enough to foul the milk vans. In the middle of the curve, it derailed through the vans, scattering them like matchwood, and ended up on its side against the tender of the 0-6-0. The 4-4-0s tender jack-knifed onto the cab, killing the crew instantly, and all the carriages were reduced to a jumble of splintered timber on the engines. Over half the passengers perished in this carnage, 24 in all. The time was 1.57 am.

An urgent message was immediately sent to Dugald at Surbiton and he sprang into action, summoning 'The Bug' and his outdoor assistant, F.C. French. They were on the scene shortly after daybreak with Dugald supervising the locomotive recovery. No. 421 had much superficial damage, the chimney had been torn off, the front safety valve was gone, the front buffer beam bent almost out of recognition and the smokebox door badly dented. The cranes which had arrived restored the battered engine to the track. The fact that, once a temporary buffer beam had been fixed into place, it was possible to tow the engine to Nine Elms for repair testifies to the sturdiness of Drummond designs.

The driver, W.J. Robins, was an experienced man, a teetotaller, and nothing untoward in the locomotive controls could be found. Robins knew the road well and the inquiry into this accident failed to find a cause, but it is significant that firstly, driver Robins had never taken a train through Salisbury non-stop before and, secondly the LSWR never again ran non-stop through Salisbury. All trains were henceforth booked to stop there. One significant feature appeared to have been glossed over, this being the higher centre of gravity of the 'L12', which was essentially a 'T9' with a bigger boiler. The boiler centre line of the 'T9' was pitched at 7 ft 9 in. above the rails, whereas the 'L12' (and 'S11') had a bigger and heavier boiler pitched at 8 ft 6 in. It is not surprising that the higher centre of gravity caused the locomotive to tip over when travelling at double the safe speed over the stretch of track in question. A 'T9' might have stayed on the rails in such a situation. Dugald also speedily issued strict orders that all specials

This photograph of the Salisbury crash shows how badly damaged were the coaches of the express.   *John Scott-Morgan Collection*

'L12' No. 427 as built stands ready for duty.   *John Scott-Morgan Collection*

Urie wasted no time in superheating the 'L12s' and removing the annoying (to the firemen) cross water tubes in the firebox. Here No. 425 is found at Salisbury on 19th July, 1924.

R.C. Stumpf/John Scott-Morgan Collection

'L12' No. 415 in original condition in Nine Elms shed, 10th April, 1920.

John Scott-Morgan Collection

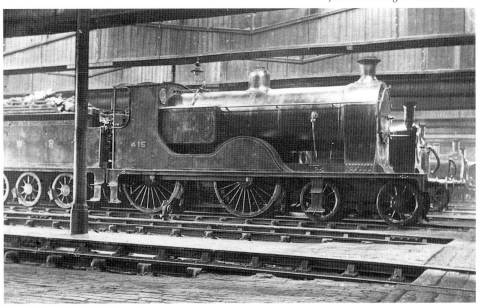

The differences between the Adams and Drummond 'B4' 0-4-0T are seen in this photograph. No. 81 *Jersey*, the first of the class was built in 1893 by the former and *Cherbourg*, No. 98, in 1900 by the latter. *Jersey* has, however, been given a Drummond chimney.   *John Scott-Morgan Collection*

Although originally built in 1891 by Adams, the 'B4' 0-4-0T was added to by Dugald Drummond. Here No. 85 of that year has been rebuilt with Drummond fittings; seen at Southampton Docks.   *John Scott-Morgan Collection*

must run to the schedule times. Up to this event the LSWR had only killed two passengers in the last 17 years.

It was in 1905 that Dugald's title of Locomotive Superintendent was altered to that of Chief Mechanical Engineer. Many other railways were adopting that title for their Superintendents, so this change was inevitable. His duties and responsibilities hardly changed, it would have been a courageous Board which would meddle with them!

Bar the 'C8' and 'K10', all Drummond 4-4-0s had a driving and coupled wheelbase of 10 feet, so a common coupling rod could be employed. Further standardisation extended to the motion parts and boilers. All 4-4-0s except the 'C8' and 'D15' had common motion and for the 'M7', '700' and all 4-4-0s save the 'D15' just two boiler/firebox combinations sufficed with minor differences only affecting the tube layout. Interchangeability between several hundred locomotives therefore helped on spares and eased manufacturing costs due to quantity production and common tooling.

Many of the Drummond 4-4-0s were capable of fast, steady, running, which was, according to Dugald, put down to the fact that he specified the bogie centre pivot point was located two inches out of centre longitudinally, presumably in a forward sense, to prevent oscillation at speed.

Whilst the 4-4-0 developments were at their peak, tragedy was to beset Dugald and the family in 1905, for in that year Walter grew ill and was diagnosed with a tumour on the pancreas, in other words, cancer. The diagnosis was not good and, leaving George in Glasgow, he and wife Elizabeth together with seven-year-old daughter Elizabeth moved down to Surbiton to be near London and its specialists, living at 'Morven' with his parents. Although not certain, it seems that Dugald, mindful of the earlier losses all those years ago at Inverness, was fiercely determined to do all possible to try and keep Walter around. Matters steadily deteriorated and Walter eventually returned to Glasgow for a last-ditch operation on the 27th June. He died shortly after, on 8th July, aged 36. This loss must have hit Dugald very hard, for now George was the sole surviving son in his family.

As with the continued production of Adams' locomotives when he arrived on the LSWR, Dugald showed his recognition of his predecessor's design abilities in not being averse to bringing out more of his designs if they suited the requirement. It made economic sense to add to existing fleets, shed staffs and crews were familiar with the types and spares could be used from existing stocks. A case in point was the 'K14' 0-4-0T. Adams had designed such a type for shunting duties, the 'B4' class, and 20 were built between 1891 and 1893. So useful did these powerful little locomotives prove that Dugald had a further five built in 1908. Most of the originals were on dock work where their 7 ft wheelbase suited the tight curves that abounded in such an environment. The five new arrivals, differing only in slightly altered dimensions and Drummond style boiler mountings, went straight to docks work. All, including the Adams variants, lasted into BR days.

Despite his own lack of technical qualification opportunities in his early days as an apprentice, Dugald realised that, out of the apprentices of the day at Nine Elms, there were some individuals who had considerable potential for the future. Accordingly, he arranged that the LSWR have a part-time course set up for them at the nearby Battersea College of Technology. This course was for two mornings a week over a three-year period, and was the start of 'sandwich courses' which proved so successful that, to this day, they continue in the University of Surrey and elsewhere. Each morning's work commenced at 8.00 am and the attendance rarely fell below 75 per cent. After three years those apprentices who showed promise could continue onto a more advanced course available in the evenings. Quite a substantial number of those eligible elected to do so.

In his early discussions with the College Dugald dealt with, and clearly appreciated, the interest of the principal, Mr Sidney H. Wells, who was a Whitworth Scholar and A.M.I.C.E. and A.M.I.Mech.E. Mr Wells and Drummond liased on the course content and clearly a mutual respect grew between the two of them. When Mr Wells left the College in 1907, Dugald purchased and presented the Wells Gold Medal to the College. This medal was to be presented annually to the best Mechanical Engineering student of the year.

For Dugald to be able to discuss matters surrounding the teaching of complex engineering subjects clearly shows an agile mind at work. Although his education had never encompassed much in the way of the theoretical matters pertaining to engineering, he obviously had collected a mass of useful and practical features associated with it during his career. Had he enjoyed a more comprehensive grounding in matters theoretical during his training, one is led to speculate whether superheating would have been entertained with more enthusiasm when it began to appear elsewhere. The steam dryers which appeared were never really effective, but were cheap. It seems strange that a man keen on fitting all sorts of gadgets to his locomotives could not go one step further and add one more. Robert Urie would often have to deflect enginemen's and shed staff's complaints about the complexities of inaccessible fittings such as steam reversers, front tube-plate clack boxes, duplex feed pumps, etc. He patiently waited for the opportunity to dispense with many of them, an opportunity which finally came after Dugald had passed away.

So far as the method of selection for premium apprentices on the railway in general went this was biased towards candidates who were related to railway employees. Pupilages, however, seemed to be more allied to the ability of parents to pay the annual fees demanded of them by the CME. Dugald was careful in his selection of both categories but happy enough to let Robert Urie deputise for him on occasion, for the premium apprentices anyway. It was of great assistance if a member of the family of the prospective apprentice knew people in high places for a personal guarantee. The fees were usually £150 per year for pupils and a one-off £50 for premiums.

Chapter Eight

Carriages, Railcars and Eastleigh

As the space at the old Nine Elms carriage shops had been needed for expansion of the locomotive works a site at Eastleigh, near Southampton, was selected and purchased for the erection of a new works. In 1891 this had been opened with the Carriage & Wagon Superintendent and practically his entire workforce transferred down there.

When Dugald appeared on the LSWR, carriage affairs had been in the capable hands of C&W Superintendent W. Panter for six years. Panter had begun replacing many of the older four- and six-wheeled vehicles with bogie stock and was beginning to introduce some unique tri-composites for the West of England services that required through carriages on the principal expresses to many destinations. He had also introduced third class bogie stock, a rarity in those days.

By the late 1890s the LSWR carriage stock was in reasonable order and could be almost equated in terms of comfort with that of the Midland Railway. Panter had come to the LSWR in 1890 from the Wolverton works of the LNWR, where the traditions in material quality and constructional soundness was excellent, and made sure these precepts were adopted on his designs.

Dugald was content to let the carriage side of things be catered for by Panter, who retired in 1906, after getting matters at Eastleigh well settled. The new Carriage Superintendent, Surrey Warner, came from the GWR works at Swindon. Warner took stock of the situation and immediately started a programme of increasing the LSWR stock of corridor coaches which were not too commonplace at that time.

Much of the older corridor stock was still without end gangways, but the new designs coming from Warner had these added, thus permitting access to dining cars from the other coaches. One new feature to appear in all new carriage stock of the 20th century of both Panter and Warner was electric lighting. The first Panter stock incorporating this was a batch of 140 four-coach bogie block sets for the extensive suburban services around London. Warner took this system into the new corridor stock he was designing and started to reduce the dependency on gas lighting with its inherent dangers in the event of an accident. He was, in fact, never to design a coach employing gas lighting for the LSWR. Dugald took note of the introduction of the new lighting and some measurements were made of the increased resistance caused by the dynamo drives. The estimates showed values roughly equal to that caused by adding an extra coach to an average eight-coach train. This, plus more luxurious and thus heavier coaches, pointed to the need for future locomotive designs to provide more power. Dugald began thinking about providing that by increasing the number of driving wheels, in other words a 4-6-0 layout. Warner continued the block set theme with four-coach lavatory sets for the semi-fast main line services.

The introduction of steam heating for passenger trains commenced in 1900 on the LSWR when a batch of 26 new bogie corridor coaches emerged from

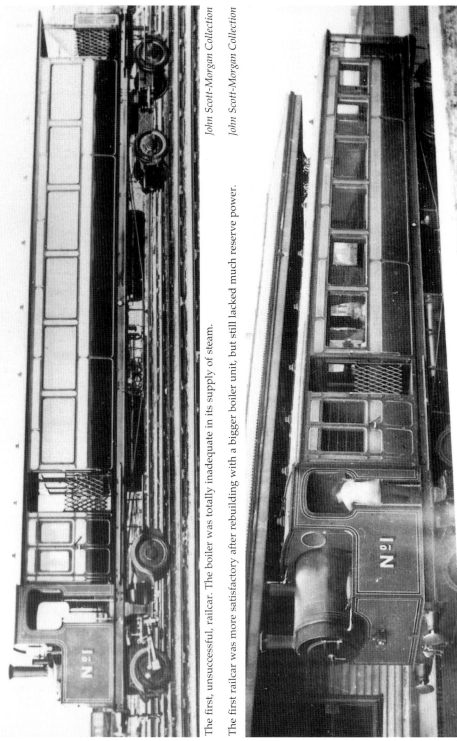

The first, unsuccessful, railcar. The boiler was totally inadequate in its supply of steam.

John Scott-Morgan Collection

The first railcar was more satisfactory after rebuilding with a bigger boiler unit, but still lacked much reserve power.

John Scott-Morgan Collection

Eastleigh carriage works. These were intended for express use on the Waterloo-Exeter run and were, as an incentive to attract regular travellers, fitted with steam heating. A number of 'T9' 4-4-0s were also fitted for supplying the necessary steam. They were put into service in early 1901 and some measurements of the effect this new equipment had on the locomotives' performance estimated that fuel consumption was increased by some 6,052 tons over the year on these services. Even with coal at a little over 15s. per ton, the £4,500 this represented resulted in some Directors querying the need for the luxury of heating. However, when a carefully measured series of tests were carried out under Dugald's guidance, it was found that a more representative figure was £1,260 per year. The engine crews were astute men and knew full well if they limited heating to the time standing prior to commencing a trip and at times when running down banks, the use of steam and thus firing of coal would be minimised. Plus of course, throughout the warmer months no heating would be necessary. When this was reported to the Board, further expansion of this facility was authorised and, by the end of 1906, all LSWR coaches were so equipped.

Apart from major matters involving the Board such as the previous example, Dugald only kept a watching brief on carriage developments over his time of office, realising that in both Panter and Warner he had extremely competent superintendents to manage matters on his behalf. One particular project which came along at the turn of the century was the steam railcar, or rail motor. Competition in some areas from electric trams was raising its head, threatening some of the small branches in and around populated areas with its frequent services. What was needed was a 'cheap train', as C. Hamilton Ellis put it. Dugald called in the Carriage Superintendent, Panter, and together they designed a double bogie steam-powered carriage. One bogie consisted of a small 0-2-2 locomotive, the driving wheels powered by 7 in. x 10 in. cylinders, the motion for which was the first application on the LSWR of Walschaert's valve gear.

Two such cars were built in 1903 and given the class designation 'K11'. Underpowered, they were soon rebuilt in 1904 with larger boilers. The only positive thing to come out of this exercise was the loaning of one to the GWR for trials on the Stroud branch line. It appears that the GWR was impressed by the experiment, for it went ahead on its own after these trials and designed and built its own design. The first of these appeared about six months after the Stroud experiment and by 1908 no fewer than 99 were in service. Churchward clearly succeeded where Drummond failed, for many of these GWR units remained in service until the 1930s.

One feature which afflicted the Drummond railcars was the frequent occurrence of hot boxes, caused by the inside bearings to all wheels being undersized. All too often one would be pulled out of service for attention to this defect. One day at Fratton the affected car was jacked up for treatment to the offending item. As it was being lowered back, the jacks on one side were let down too fast, and the whole assembly fell over on its side. Alerted to this, Drummond summoned the 'Bug' and went post-haste to Fratton, got out and viewed the scene. For once, he was bereft of words at the sad sight, remounted

The class 'H13' railcars looked workmanlike, but the addition of another trailer taxed the small engines to their limit. They quickly fell out of use and were converted to push-pull trailers.
John Scott-Morgan Collection

The destination board can just be made out to read 'Bodmin' on this railcar, but unfortunately the number is not legible. *R.S. Carpenter Collection*

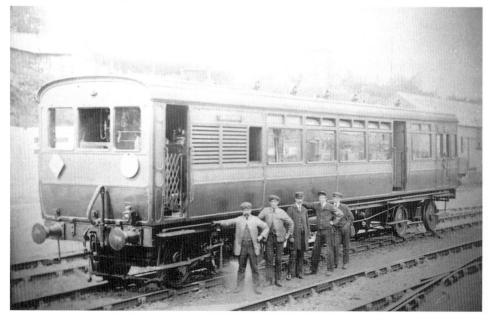

his steed and drove off. The casualty was righted, repaired and put back into service on the Southsea run. From Drummond's office there remained a dignified silence.

Despite the early disappointments, Dugald persisted and by 1906 fifteen more rail motors had appeared and were distributed over the system. The first two, class 'H12', were different in that the engine portion was totally enclosed in a metal box blended into the carriage body of the vehicle. The design had one further iteration with a final batch of 13, class 'H13', which had a better styling of the engine portion. Most were out of service by 1916 and all had gone by 1919. The coach bodies were converted into push-and-pull trailers, being used for many years.

Following the disappointing performance with the railcars a batch of small 2-2-0Ts, class 'C14', was authorised. Intended for push and pull trains, they were far too small and suffered from lack of adhesion, being incapable of coping adequately with a single trailer. They were quickly displaced to light shunting tasks, which could even tax their limited power some times. In later years four were converted to 0-4-0Ts, two of which surprisingly lasted into BR days.

As the new century had approached, a scheme to widen the Waterloo approach lines meant that part of the Nine Elms works would have to be demolished. The Goods Department was also pressing for more space in their yard nearby and so the opportunity presented itself for the LSWR Board to consider a new locomotive works elsewhere. Dugald, at first, was hesitant about moving the works outside London, but became resigned to the fact after realising the Board's determination to carry out the Waterloo approach reordering. They had just ordered the plans for a new South station to be drawn up and purchase of the land had received the necessary powers to proceed from an Act passed in 1899.

Accordingly, in 1899 it was decided in principle to move the locomotive works to Eastleigh where some 200 acres had been bought the year previously and where the works and a new locomotive depot would be sited. Dugald, somewhat reluctantly, agreed to this plan and a start was made by him in the planning of the new facilities. Robert Urie sat in on the meetings and was delegated, eventually, to go down to Eastleigh to oversee the whole project. He would, after all, be Works Manager there.

The LSWR had, for many years now, been known as the 'Military' line, as it served both Aldershot and the military ranges on Salisbury Plain. The task of transporting the Forces of the Crown came to a head in 1899 when the Boer War began in South Africa. Between August 1899 and January 1900, the railway put on 464 special trains comprising 1,818 coaches, 259 horseboxes, 1,189 cattle wagons and 1,366 other goods vehicles, to convey 118,000 troops to Southampton for embarkation. The '700' class 0-6-0s were used on many of these trains.

The onset of the Boer War ignited a flame in Dugald's patriotic heart, for he had always shown great interest in the Engineer and Railway Volunteer Corps, which several of the other railways had encouraged following a proposal of Charles Manby, the Secretary of the Institution of Civil Engineers, in 1864. This proposal had been for an organization for the directing of railway transport and

No. 741, of the 'C14' class, has been converted from 2-2-0T to 0-4-0T and is at work in Southampton Docks on 15th April, 1922. *John Scott-Morgan Collection*

The first locomotive to be turned out of the new Eastleigh works was this little 0-4-0T of class 'S14'. Only two were ever built and were sold in 1917 to the Ministry of Munitions. No. 101 depicted here lasted until 1944, having had a repair at Derby in 1940.

John Scott-Morgan Collection

Dugald Drummond in his Volunteers (Railway Engineers) uniform. Doubtless his forthright
manner suited the military sphere.   *John Scott-Morgan Collection*

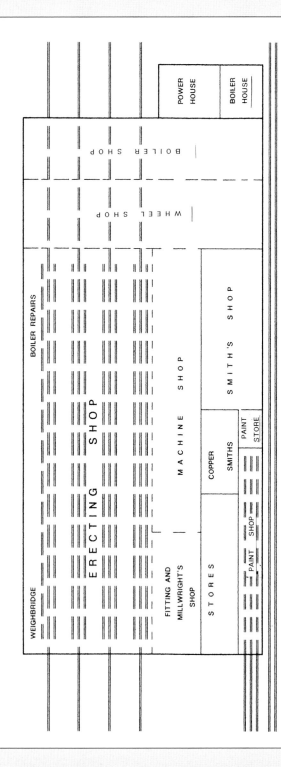

EASTLEIGH LOCOMOTIVE WORKS AS SET OUT BY ROBERT URIE

Author

labour to the work of National Defence in times of emergency. Dugald involved himself personally in the Corps formed on the LSWR, being granted the rank of Major. No back seat for him, he intended leading from the front.

The ARLE held a meeting on 24th November, 1899 as the LSWR was busy transporting all the military supplies to the ports. Dugald was among the 29 members who attended. Matters dealt with revolved around firebox stays, with Harry Pollitt of the Great Central Railway stating his preference for the flexible type then being fitted on 40 of his new engines under construction.

November 1900, as many troop trains were passing on their way to Southampton Docks, saw the beginning of work on the new locomotive depot, which would eventually replace that at Northam on the outskirts of Southampton. It was not until January 1903 that it was ready for occupation. By this date construction of the works had only just started and this proceeded fitfully as each stage required separate authorisation. There was much to do in connection with this development, for all the staff at Nine Elms were to be transferred to Eastleigh and housing would be required. Much of the machine tools at Nine Elms were to be moved down there and a huge logistic programme to achieve this in a short space of time would be needed.

Dugald and Urie were, between them, to mastermind this transfer, with Urie's calm and ordered mind placing priorities on Dugald's sharp commands. Many times 'The Bug' could be seen scurrying down the main line with a pair of heads inside poring over plans.

The opportunity to build a new works from scratch was a great chance for Dugald to put into practice what he had hoped for in the existing works, but had been restricted by limits posed by available space. The Eastleigh plant as laid out by him was to be spacious with wide bays to permit easy movement and, importantly, with an eye to future expansion. No more would cramped conditions be allowed to have an adverse effect on production and repair work.

Some housing was in place by the end of 1904, but this was immediately taken by the enginemen transferred from Northam. As matters progressed on the works, some staff began to appear in 1909 to begin setting up the first of the machines from Nine Elms. They found no housing, for the LSWR Board had decided to place that provision in the hands of private builders. This had delayed the completion of the promised accommodation. As the opening date of January 1910 approached, the LSWR approved the construction of 100 cottages nearby, which were not completed until November 1912. Early days at Eastleigh were not all that happy for the 1,500 men transferred with their families.

Whilst Eastleigh was being planned and built much time was spent down there on the site by the CME, who arranged that a specially reserved timing path be made available in the morning and evening between Surbiton and Eastleigh. 'The Bug' was run at express speeds on these trips, a feature which appeared to be enjoyed by Dugald, for on several occasions he was known to hint to the driver to let the little locomotive have its head. The stability of this unit at speeds over 80 mph was a little lacking and it tended to hunt from side to side considerably. On one occasion an old Scottish colleague from the Highland Railway was being brought back from a visit to Eastleigh and the 23½ miles from Basingstoke to Woking was covered in 16½ minutes, an average speed of 85 mph! The HR man eventually became so unnerved by the antics of the machine that he struggled to the hatchway and implored the driver to moderate his speed. Dugald sat impassive, clearly enjoying his friend's discomfort, knowing that very soon they would be slowing for the approach to Hampton Court Junction and Surbiton.

At the half-yearly meeting in February 1910, the LSWR Chairman, Sir Charles Scotter, reported that the CME had stated:

> The locomotive works at Nine Elms are now closed and the men and machinery are removed to Eastleigh. The works are designed to reduce to the minimum the handling of material, and the process of manufacture and the machinery are the finest that can be procured for our requirements. This transfer has been accomplished without an employee of the department being one hour out of work or the output of the work interfered with. I have no hesitation in saying that the company possesses the most complete and up-to-date works owned by any railway company.

Altogether an impressive statement, but just how such a major upheaval of a manufacturing concern can take place without any hours out of work for the employees is a mystery. There must have been an allowance of time to cater for the disruption caused which was offset for being non-productive.

As an exercise in logistics, the move to Eastleigh was a classic piece of organization by Dugald and his team. Towards the end of 1909, as Nine Elms began to run down, there were almost nightly special trains conveying the machinery and equipment down for reinstallation in the new premises. And so, in 1910, the new works were commissioned, except for the office block which would contain the technical departments, which opened later the same year.

The new works were laid out such that the hot and dusty conditions of the foundries and forge were in separate buildings from the other shops. Erection, boiler, fitting, machine and paint shops were all under one roof in the main building, with adequate travelling cranes of high capacities installed. All the larger machines had their own independent drives and, where required, pneumatic hoists to assist their loading. The erecting shop comprised four large bays, one for large engines, another for small to medium, a third for building new engines and a fourth had part of one end devoted to tender and boiler repairs. Drummond and Urie planned the layout to ensure that space was available so that the handling of large components into place could be carried out with little or no interference with other operations going on nearby. Advantage was taken to equip the machine shop with the very latest in new turret lathes, milling machines, wheel lathes etc. to increase the productivity. The resulting works, when opened, was a model of efficient working practices and became a show-piece for the LSWR. It was, however, completely lacking in any heating whatsoever, as though Dugald had decreed that 'working will keep them warm'. Whilst summer conditions were pleasant, some of the winter months must have been uncomfortable in the extreme.

One particular change in working practices was the alteration to working hours of 50 per week, made up of 7.00 am-12.00 noon and 1.00-5.00 pm shifts on Mondays to Fridays plus a 7.00 am-12 noon Saturday shift. The change from the old 6 am start, with a breakfast break, was much appreciated by the workforce.

Despite being the most up-to-date works in terms of working practices and equipment, Eastleigh still fell short of many features which today would raise the hackles of the factory inspectors. For instance, the toilet facilities were basic and wash-basins few and far between. To rid their hands of ingrained grime the works' employees had to oil them, then wash the congealed mess off in paraffin before finalising the procedure with soap and hot water usually heated by the nearest riveter on his little hand-blown forge. No barrier creams and no washrooms with plenty of hot water in those days!

Dugald did not move down to that area, he continued to live at Surbiton, where 'The Bug' called on an almost daily basis to shuttle him down to Eastleigh or up to Waterloo as circumstances dictated. He was now 70, yet showed no signs of wishing to retire, being absorbed in sorting through the changes to his 4-6-0 developments.

So far as integrating with the workforce as a whole, Dugald had become involved with the LSWR Engineering Society quite early on and was inevitably elected as its President. At each of the Annual Meetings he would give an address, usually concerning railway matters, it being a good forum for passing down his thoughts and plans for current developments and design aspects of his locomotives. The 1911 meeting was notable for some relevant comments on design features of locomotives under the title 'Things to Know and Avoid in the Design and Management of the Modern Locomotive Engine'.

Dugald started by being critical of the move to adopt American management methods on the railways which, in his opinion, overlooked the fact that the operating and other conditions were entirely different in that land. He also referred to recent imports of locomotives from the USA which, to his mind, were much inferior to their British counterparts. The Midland Railway, in particular, had, in a time of locomotive shortage, imported a batch of American 2-6-0s to fill the urgent need for motive power. Not much from across the Atlantic seemed to come up to his own management and engineering standards. This critical appraisal was wound up by an attack on the adoption of the 4-4-2 Atlantic by some railways by listing it as 'the most unsatisfactory engine that has ever been introduced into English practice'. He also criticised the Atlantic as being hard on track and bridges when compared to four-cylinder six-coupled types. Presumably he was talking about two-cylinder 4-4-2s, which were, like any balanced two-cylinder engine with counter-balance weight on the wheels, prone to high axle loads at speed due to hammer blow, not a very fair comparison.

On superheating he was of the opinion that a steam temperature of 450°F was adequate enough and most certainly that 600°F advocated by others was excessive.

Robert Urie transferred his Works Manager's post to Eastleigh, concentrating on the completion of the offices, which would eventually house his own staff as well as the drawing office, which was still led by J.A. Hunter, an Aberdonian drafted in by Dugald. The new 4-6-0s were still giving problems and he had his own ideas for the remedies needed, but a stubborn boss who brooked no interference in his designs blocked all efforts in that area.

LECTURES

ON THE

WORKING OF

LOCOMOTIVE ENGINES

BY

D. DRUMMOND, M.I.C.E.

Sold for the Benefit of the
London & South Western Railway Servants' Orphanage.

'G14' class 4-6-0 No. 453 is illustrated on the front cover of the pamphlet *Lectures on the working of Locomotive Engines* by Dugald Drummond.

Chapter Nine

The 4-6-0s, a final 4-4-0 and an Untimely End

The 1905 summer meeting of the ARLE, which was attended by Dugald, took place at the Imperial Hotel, Torquay. The main subject tabled for this gathering was: 'Proposals for the [medical] examination of old enginemen'. A series of draft rules for consideration were put to those assembled, viz:

(a) All enginemen over the age of 60 should have annual medical checks.
(b) If in good health they could go on to 70, unless employed on long non-stop runs, when 65 would be the retiring age.
(c) If in failing health they should be put onto less important work.
(d) Heart disease or varicose veins (why only these two afflictions is a mystery) would result in immediate removal from the footplate.
(e) To keep a check on eyesight meant regular examinations would be required (presumably irrespective of age).
(f) With regard to eyesight, enginemen between 55 and 60 showing signs of deterioration should be dealt with as if they were over 60.

The discussion that ensued from these suggested criteria was long and varied. Dugald said it was difficult to draw a hard and fast line. He did not care to have drivers over 55 on express trains; 'although if they are in good health and possess sound eyesight, they are fit for lighter employment until they qualify for superannuating at 60'. Right throughout Dugald's career we find the practical side coming out in his dealings with the crews under him.

Here, certainly, is a man who took care to assess the fitness of his footplate staff. After all, it was they who were responsible for large numbers of passengers and trains conveying sometimes valuable and urgent freight upon which the railway depended for its income and, ultimately, profitability. Dugald clearly recognised their importance and was determined to ensure that their services were kept at a high level of efficiency. It is not surprising that he was so irate when a misdemeanour by some individual footplate staff came to his notice, or even cropped up in his presence. His explosive manner of dealing with such miscreants was, to him, a normal reaction to wrong-doing. Sometimes, this made matters worse, for example the poor passed fireman backing a locomotive towards an incorrectly set turntable froze in terror at the frenzied shouts and gestures of Drummond trying to warn him. Needless to say, the end result was a derailment into the turntable pit and an instantly demoted (back to fireman) member of the footplate staff!

Dugald had started on the shop floor as an apprentice craftsman and had extensive experience of production methods from the workman's point of view. He clearly could converse with the foremen in the works in their own language, which itself earned a lot of respect, albeit with appropriate deference. In addition, his knowledge of locomotive handling, both in terms of firing and driving, was considerable, as we have seen, in the writing of the booklet of lectures covering the management of their engines. He had taken no financial gain from this publication, it being sold for the benefit of the LSWR servants' orphanage.

It was this practical side of Drummond that kept him in touch with his men and he especially took note of the younger elements. These were the ones from whose ranks would come future key personnel. To that end he ordered that classes in the works be established to train them further in their skills.

His mode of dress hardly changed, such that he was instantly recognisable on his inspection tours. A black raincoat or overcoat incorporating an Inverness cape and a black boiler hat were the norm. A sharp eye was often kept for the familiar attire should it be known that 'The Bug' was on the road.

So much has been passed down about Dugald Drummond's outspoken and harsh manner of dealing with those brought before him for 'carpeting'. He probably knew his men better than many of their immediate superiors and it is refreshing to come across a spark of humanity within those fierce and withering sentences dealt out to miscreants. The following is a typical example.

A driver at Salisbury was reported for running through a signal set at danger and duly summoned to explain himself, if he could, in Dugald's office. This man readily admitted his error and offered no excuse. Dugald pressed him further, did the fireman distract him or was smoke obscuring the signals? Neither of these, or other possibilities, had, and the driver agreed that signals were to be obeyed at all times. Puzzled by this frank admission as to his carelessness, Drummond probed further, asking was anything amiss at home? The driver mentioned that he had just suffered the loss of one of his children and that another was seriously ill, but that was no excuse for his misdemeanour.

'Man', growled Drummond, clearly remembering his own tragic losses at Inverness and how they affected himself, 'you're exonerated'.

It was little actions such as this that earned him the respect of many of the enginemen. He may have had a tough exterior, but he also clearly had an underlying streak of human understanding when needed, plus a willingness to take the trouble to investigate further if he sensed that other factors might be involved.

One great attribute of Drummond designs was the emphasis placed on the standardisation of parts. So many of the 4-4-0s had common motion parts, for instance, that any repairs in that area were quickly accomplished using stocks of spares readily available. All this led to low maintenance costs which helped to keep the overall cost of running the railway at an acceptable level. The commonality, we have seen, also spread across to boiler/firebox assemblies, cylinder block castings and many sundry fittings so far as locomotives were concerned. Likewise many classes shared tenders. The big break with all this came when the four-cylinder 4-6-0s appeared with their Walschaert's valve gear, outside cylinders and new boilers.

Further economies were to be found in the type of axle-boxes employed. Not those lined with anti-friction white metal, but bronze machined castings originally, before the change to forged steel boxes with fitted brass liners. These last ones, although more expensive to manufacture, could at least be case-hardened, as could the axle-box cheeks on the frames. This gave good wearing properties again helping towards lengthening the servicing intervals, thus lowering costs over a maintenance cycle.

The genesis of the Dugald Drummond 4-6-0s was sparked off in 1903 following a visit by him, at the invitation of McIntosh, to St Rollox. Upon arrival at his old stamping ground he was taken to view the latest express type, a 4-6-0. The story goes that he, after querying the need for such a large locomotive, returned to Nine Elms and immediately set the drawing office on the design of the first of a family of 4-6-0s.

Dugald's 4-6-0s were a series of large but, in the early days at least, not very successful attempts at introducing this wheel arrangement on the LSWR. His brother Peter had, in 1900, brought out a 4-6-0 on the Highland Railway which was to prove very successful, but this was based on a Jones design study of an upgrade to his earlier 'Jones Goods' 4-6-0. Dugald's first effort appeared in 1905 with a batch of five for mixed traffic work, the 'F13' class.

The 'F13', like all Drummond 4-6-0s for the LSWR was a massive locomotive, in some respects rather reminiscent of an enlarged 4-2-2-0. The disposition of the cylinders, those inside well forward driving the front axle and those outside behind the leading bogie driving the middle coupled axle gave this impression.

As with most of the 4-4-0s, the boiler had firebox watertubes and a steam reverser was employed, as were the feed-water heater and feed pumps. Also, as for the 4-2-2-0s, the inside and outside valve gears were dissimilar, this time Stephenson inside and Walschaert's outside. The ashpan lay between the rear pair of coupled wheels and was rather limited in volume for the large firebox as a result. This long and shallow firebox, with the cross watertubes, proved almost impossible to fire adequately and steaming suffered accordingly. A series of tests with two firemen feeding specially selected quality coal produced a reasonably satisfactory performance, but of course this could not be justified in service.

Initially these monsters were put onto express work by Dugald but persistently poor performance had them all relegated to goods work within a year of operation, their normal task being on Royal Navy coal trains from Wales to Portsmouth, which they took over from the GWR *en route*.

An example of a slightly revised version of the 'F13' appeared in 1905, the 'E14'. This had a modified Walschaert's gear on the outside driving piston valves. The tender was also fitted with water pick-up equipment for the planned water troughs which, in fact, were never installed on the LSWR. Some surveys at Fleet and Abbey Ford near Templecombe had been carried out, these being two places where over a mile of track was level. However, since the Salisbury accident, the mandatory stop made there for all trains at which water could be taken on, probably negated the need for troughs. For some reason the 'E14' exhibited a huge coal consumption, being given the nickname of the 'Turkey' due to this coal gobbler feature. This poor performer was soon laid aside and rarely entered traffic, as Dugald had decided that modifications were needed, but none had materialised by the time he died and it was left to Urie to withdraw and replace this single example.

None of these first two classes of 4-6-0 could be encouraged to run fast. Sluggish to the last, they eventually went into storage. The 'F13s' lived on into SR days, being scrapped in 1924 by Maunsell, who used some components of them in the construction of five 'H15s' at that time. The single 'E14' had been

The first 4-6-0 of the 'F13' class, No. 330 in as-built condition.   *John Scott-Morgan Collection*

'F13' No. 333 at Exeter *c.*1910. This particular example was superheated by Urie, a modification which gave no improvement.   *John Scott-Morgan Collection*

'F13' No. 332 in storage at Eastleigh on 17th September, 1922. Two further years were to
elapse before final scrapping.   *John Scott-Morgan Collection*

similarly dealt with as early as 1914, so this indicated Urie's opinion of that
design. Had the World War not intervened, doubtless the same fate would have
been vested on the 'F13s', but the urgent need for motive power, no matter how
poor the quality, certainly lengthened their lives.

The relegation to freight duties of the 'F13s' effectively put paid to what
would have been a radical new design for the LSWR. Concurrent to the 4-6-0s
design, Dugald had the drawing office scheming a freight 0-8-0 which used the
boiler assembly of the 'F13'. It also had four cylinders, but this time all in line,
plus a divided drive to the second and third axles. Six had, in fact, been planned
and a case for the order considered, when the reasonable success of the 'F13s'
on freight work resulted in the cessation of this scheme. The story of the 0-8-0
has, in fact, been subject to some conflicting reports as to its date. The Eastleigh
drawing register held at the NRM carries a reference to an eight-coupled
locomotive drawing in October 1912. Other references have quoted a 1905/6
date for a first sketch, but no drawing reference, which then would have been
Nine Elms, is to be found. One plausible scenario is that, around 1905, as the
'F13' was being introduced, Dugald had some sketches done of an 0-8-0,
spurred on by the knowledge of Peter's 0-8-0 project of 1902 for the HR. These
were put aside once the 'F13s' were relegated to freight traffic duties, effectively
squashing any argument for a specialised freight type. This 0-8-0 scheme of
Dugald's then reappears in 1912 and was actually given an order number -
'H15'. The sudden death of Dugald saw no further work on the 0-8-0, which was
cancelled and Urie converted the order into the first of his mixed-traffic 4-6-0s,
the 'H15' class, the first batch of 10 appearing in 1914. This Urie design utilised
some boiler shells already approved for the Drummond 0-8-0, hence the carry-
over of the order number used for the class designation.

Right: Dugald Drummond in 1910.

Below: Brookwood Cemetery provided an appropriate resting place for Dugald Drummond, as it was served by the London & South Western Railway. The train which conveyed his coffin to Brookwood was hauled by one of his own engines, 'D15' class 4-4-0 No. 463, on 11th November, 1912. The full story of Brookwood Cemetery and its unusual railway service can be found in *The Brookwood Necropolis Railway*, John Clarke, Oakwood Press (OL143). *John Clarke*

The regular ARLE meetings, after the one which concerned the health of enginemen, continued, but Dugald rarely, if ever, attended. New developments in locomotive detail design were appearing, to some of which he was violently opposed. Perhaps he felt that his way of doing things as regards locomotive design might be undermined if he was coerced into some changes. It took a lot of time and a determined mind to get a Drummond to change his ways.

In 1905, he had stated at the November meeting that he wished his name to be erased from the list of members. There is no record of this having been done, maybe those present thought this was a typical blunt, brief, statement which would fade into the past. Most certainly he clearly wished to follow his precepts without any outside influences or criticisms.

By 1908, Dugald had completed the designs for another 4-6-0, the 'G14'. This had a smaller boiler than the previous two attempts and had the first application of the Drummond approach to superheating, the infamous 'steam dryer' consisting of a clutch of pipes grouped in the smokebox through which steam passed to the steam chest and cylinders. The effect on the draughting was negative and, compounded with the long shallow firebox, made satisfactory steaming difficult to maintain. Five were built in total and were used on mixed traffic duties between Salisbury and Exeter, where they performed only reasonably well. Like their elder cousins the 'F13' they were withdrawn in SR days in the mid-1920s.

The moderate success, and it was moderate, of the 'G14' led Dugald to modify the design and produce another batch of five, to be known as the 'P14' class. The principal changes in this batch was the provision of a longer coupled wheelbase of eight inches and the employment of piston valves. A slight improvement in performance was detected but at the expense of a large appetite for coal, which led to the nickname 'Big Gobblers'. All the 'P14s', which incorporated steam dryers, were built at Eastleigh and like the other early 4-6-0s were gone by the mid-1920s, except for one example, No. 449, used as a guinea-pig by Maunsell when experimenting with crank settings of 135 degrees proposed for the 'Lord Nelson' four-cylinder design then being schemed.

However, the one feature which was a distinct advance in the design process was the employment of piston valves. These had been introduced on other railways over the past 10-15 years and were proving to be effective steam and exhaust distributors. Dugald had clearly studied their incorporation elsewhere and came up with some basic rules for the design office. These specified that a recommended diameter should be 0.6 of the cylinder diameter or, alternatively their area ⅓ of the piston area. All his remaining express designs were to incorporate piston valves.

Of the earlier 4-6-0s, which had outside cylinders fitted well back in relation to those inside, some frame troubles manifested themselves due to the inadequacy of the frame stays. These were stressed to their limit by the strains set up due to piston thrusts of the widely-spaced cylinder locations. Fairly constant remedial work was needed to stiffen the stay attachments. Dugald noted this deficiency and, in the final 'T14' class 4-6-0, changed the cylinder location to that of all in line at the smokebox, which effectively eliminated the problem. This was an easy design change to implement as it had already been schemed for the cancelled 0-8-0.

'T14' No. 444 passes Surbiton *c*.1912/14.   *John Scott-Morgan Collection*

'T14' No. 447 approaches Surbiton on a lengthy down express. The absence of a third rail dates this to pre-1915.   *John Scott-Morgan Collection*

This final Drummond 4-6-0, the 'T14' was to prove the most successful of the series. This was built for express work on the Bournemouth line and had 6 ft 7 in. wheels instead of the 6 ft ones of the preceding 4-6-0s. The outside cylinders, having been moved forward to a position where they were in-line with the inside cylinders, did result in a rather bulky front end with the outside cylinders and piston valves blended into a wide casing which was a continuation of the smokebox casing. The valve gear also differed in that the outside Walschaert's motion drove the inside valves through rocking levers. Ten emerged from Eastleigh in 1911 and served tolerably well on their allotted tasks, although having so great a thirst that almost immediately a special set of tenders of 5,800 gallon capacity had to be provided. The original 4,500 gallon units were totally inadequate. The large continuous splashers over the coupled wheels eventually led to them being dubbed 'Paddleboats', as these appendages reminded so many of the Isle of Wight paddle steamers at that time in use between the mainland and the island.

Alone of the five variants of Drummond 4-6-0s, the 'T14' was considered to be suitable for rebuilding. Urie carried out the first such episode from 1915 onwards, by fitting superheaters which markedly reduced coal and water consumption. He also started to remove the cross water tubes in the firebox, which had long been his desire.

All these early 4-6-0s suffered from hot boxes, and this affliction was never satisfactorily resolved until Maunsell further rebuilt the last 'T14' batch in 1927 and, after this showed no improvement to the problem, fitted Wakefield mechanical lubricators in 1930.

With the indifferent performance of all these 4-6-0s, some people began to say, behind Dugald's back, that 'The Old Man' was past it. However, the final offering was yet to come, which clearly pointed to the fact that the 4-4-0 was his best offering for express and mixed traffic duties. The 0-6-0 reigned supreme for purely freight traffic, which was of relatively minor importance on the LSWR.

Despite being poor performers, the 4-6-0s were impressive locomotives and certainly gave the impression of lofty power. The remainder of his designs carried on the many tasks allotted to them reliably and safely, coping with the increasing demands put upon them. Down at Eastleigh works the production and repair cycles continued in the spacious premises laid out to give the workmen the best engineering facilities in the country. So it was quite in order for Dugald to be basking in plenty of esteem amongst the eminent locomotive engineers of the day and allocated an impressive £5,000 salary (nearly £500,000 today).

The last 4-4-0 design of Dugald's appeared in 1912, after the episode of the 4-6-0s in their various iterations. This final offering, the 'D15' class, was, perhaps, the best looking and most successful of all Drummond 4-4-0s. Two departures from earlier 4-4-0 tradition were the employment of piston valves and inside Walschaert's gear, the single eccentrics of the latter permitting very adequate bearing sizes. To obtain equivalent steaming, in terms of evaporation, from a bigger boiler, the 'D15' had a larger grate area of 27 sq. ft than the previous 4-4-0s with the 10 ft coupled wheelbase. This meant that the grate had to be raised at the rear in order to get the required extra length over the rear coupled axle. The boiler pressure was also now set at 200 lb./sq. in. The front

'T14' No. 462, built in 1912 at Eastleigh, has been superheated by Urie in 1917, also having the firebox cross water tubes removed. After this the locomotives were satisfactory enough to live on into the 1940s and 1950s.   *John Scott-Morgan Collection*

The 'T14' lasted well with rebuilds by Urie and Maunsell. Here No. 30446 looks in good working order at Eastleigh 5th September, 1948.   *John Scott-Morgan Collection*

end was a new departure from all previous locomotives in that the piston valves were arranged for outside admission. The valves, being placed on top of the cylinders, this layout gave a particularly free exhaust which contributed to the free running characteristics of this class. The 'D15' was also unique in that it was fitted with a Caledonian style hooter instead of the standard whistle. We have seen that Dugald had tried introducing this on both the 'M7' and '700' classes when they appeared but was ordered by no less that the Board to remove it and replace with the whistle they expected.

The 'D15s' were put onto the Bournemouth and Salisbury expresses and proved free runners and were generally classed as being two coaches better than the 4-6-0s. Ten were to be built in all, at Eastleigh, and the class was not quite complete before their designer met with his end.

So far as other developments taking place on the LSWR were concerned, if they were allied to locomotive operation, Dugald would have his say. Fog in and around London in particular was a continual problem on the railways and could cause considerable delays. The problem of sighting signals resulted in a hazard only negated by slower running so as to be able to brake and stop in a reasonably short distance. Dugald was well aware of this ever-present problem which had resulted in several collisions on the crowded lines into Waterloo. In 1911, he accordingly devised a system of advanced warning which employed a mechanical contact between the locomotive and a ramp on the track which was raised if the signal was at danger. When the contact took place the apparatus on the engine sounded a warning whistle in the cab and applied the brakes. A prototype set-up was installed near the LSWR signal works at Wimbledon and an engine modified, this being 'M7' No. 481, but early trials showed that the contact between locomotive and track was not always sufficient to activate the apparatus. By the time schemes to improve this were being considered, Dugald was dead and development of the pioneering Automatic Train Control quietly faded. An alternative system replacing the mechanical contact with an electrical track circuit was under test in 1913 but the advent of World War I curtailed any full development and application.

In 1912, the LSWR obtained a new General Manager in Herbert Walker. He had come from the position of outdoor goods manager on the LNWR, Southern Division. One of Walker's first orders was to initiate monthly meetings of Traffic, Commercial, CME and Running Officers at Waterloo. Walker was a shrewd character, completely without humour, an excellent judge of men and a skilled organizer. A factor which would have been on early agendas was that of electrification. The LSWR was suffering in the suburbs with competition from electric trams and Walker clearly saw the counter to that in a fast, frequent service only possible with electric trains.

How Walker and Drummond sized each other up is not clear. Dugald would have sensed that here was a General Manager who clearly meant business in bringing the LSWR into a modern and efficient shape to serve its area. Walker would have known that in Drummond he had an individual used to doing things his own way, one who needed handling very carefully. A stickler for correct train timing, Walker would have quite possibly wished to curtail the use of 'The Bug' should this interfere with scheduled services.

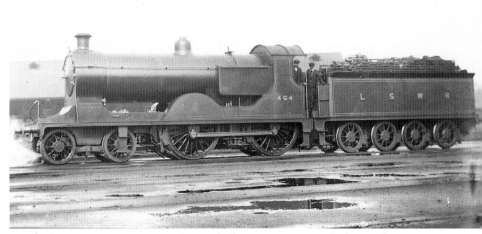

The big 4-4-0, 'D15' No. 464 displays its high boiler centre-line which gave the class its bulky looks. Sadly Dugald was not around to see his final class completed.

John Scott-Morgan Collection

'D15' No. 471 in almost ex-works condition at Bournemouth Central in late 1912, note the indicator shelter.   *R.S. Carpenter Collection*

'D15' with its BR number but still with 'SOUTHERN' on the tender; Eastleigh 28th May, 1950.
John Scott-Morgan Collection

'D15' No. 30469, Dugald Drummond's big 4-4-0 has just a few years to go and by the time of this photo, 14th July, 1950, had acquired cut-down boiler mountings and conventional safety valve postioning.   *J.M. Jarvis*

So, as 1912 advanced, two very determined men sparred with each other's desires, but the battle that might have ensued never materialised, for Dugald's time was limited.

We have seen earlier that although Dugald had indicated his wish not to remain a member of the ARLE as far back as 1905, no action had ever been taken to remove his name from the membership list. One of the last communications he had with that body was in 1912, not long before his death. The ARLE clearly had some form of rota for selecting its officers and, at the Summer meeting in 1912, it appears that Dugald's name came up for a Vice-Pesidency. Even though his non-attendance had been a fact for some seven years a communication was sent notifying him of this election. He duly wrote back declining the position.

In September 1912 an injury to one of his legs had Dugald laid up for an operation on that limb. What the injury was caused by is a bit obscure, but it has been said that it occurred through getting his feet wet one autumn day and, arriving home, demanding a mustard bath to restore some circulation in them. The initial offering, it appears was not hot enough and successive amounts of nearly boiling water was brought to remedy the situation. Scalding was the inevitable outcome, followed by inadequate care afterwards, for the damaged skin turned septic. His age and stubborn determination to continue at work despite considerable discomfort resulted in a serious deterioration into a gangrenous condition. In true Drummond form he continued to work as much as possible, in obvious discomfort, hobbling around barking orders. The 'Bug' was much in use between Surbiton and Eastleigh and in late October he was seen, quite crippled, making his way into the Eastleigh office block from the parked 'Bug'. Two weeks later, at Morven on 7th November, he was dead. Apparently, it appears that the Doctor summoned to give an opinion on the situation took one look and prescribed amputation. The shock of this further drastic treatment was too much for a man in his 73rd year. It is said he steadfastly refused an anaesthetic. He died as he would have wished, in harness. And so ended an illustrious career during which he had supplied several of the major British railways with a range of robust locomotives, which, for the majority, were long-lived and reliable.

The Locomotive Department of the LSWR had lost a controversial CME who was both admired and feared by many, loathed by some, yet in some strange way looked up to as a leader by all. The burial took place at Brookwood cemetery, just off the main line between Woking and Farnborough, along which 'The Bug' sometimes used to prowl during its 'inspection' jaunts. His coffin was carried by a group of his engine drivers from the house to the nearby Surbiton station, where it was loaded onto a special train hauled by one of the latest 4-4-0s, 'D15' No. 463, complete with its Caledonian style hooter, on his final journey over the LSWR. The story went that half a ton of brake blocks weighed down the coffin, lest its occupier should dare to rise again to vent some vitriolic comments on some enginemen's practices as they passed by.

Down at Eastleigh works on the afternoon of the funeral the warning bells rang and all work stopped. The chargehands in the machine shop turned off the power and the noise of the machines ceased. For two minutes the workforce stood respectfully in silence for Drummond before the hum and clatter of work began again. No more would he be seen on his regular inspection jaunts eyeing up the progress on his latest creation. Many years after his death, he was referred to as the 'Old Man' by the Eastleigh workforce. No other CME associated with that works ever achieved the same degree of affection as had this forthright Scot.

The frequent excursions of Dugald no longer plagued the Traffic Department, for 'The Bug' had been well employed over its 12-year term of use by the CME. Mileages for it quoted vary between 171,000 and 361,000 in those years. The correct figure is difficult to discern from these two widely differing values, but a weekly mileage of 120 between Surbiton and Nine Elms would have been feasible, whilst for the Eastleigh trips this could rise to over 900 if daily visits were made. Given a 6-day week for 50 weeks a year with 10 years to and from Nine Elms and Eastleigh, the latter on frequent visits to check on progress, and two years to and from Eastleigh almost daily, gives a total of over 220,000 miles to and from work. The extra miles on the less frequent inspection trips seem a bit excessive to reach 361,000 miles, so the author's guess is for something between the quoted figures, but biased towards the higher value. A figure of 361,000 almost equates to 12 years to and from Eastleigh every day, which is clearly not possible as that site only operated as a complete works from 1910.

Robert Urie settled into the vacant CME post effortlessly. He had been waiting in the wings for some years by now and had his own ideas as to the design of 4-6-0s, which had been largely kept to himself, for he well knew that Dugald would have dismissed them outright. He was, in a few years, to transform the fleet of large locomotives of the LSWR and lay a solid foundation for Maunsell to build upon after Grouping in 1923, but that is another story. His aim was of making matters easier for shed staff and paying great attention to standardisation of components. He had no use for 'The Bug' and it lay neglected in the inner confines of Eastleigh works for many years, only occasionally coming out for special trips locally, its last recorded duties being to haul a special saloon around Southampton Docks in 1932. The firebox eventually showed signs of collapse and the vehicle was condemned in 1940, the engine portion being cut up, the saloon serving as a grounded body at Eastleigh works for some years. This relic can now be found preserved in the garden of the Chairman of the Drummond Locomotive Society at Swanage.

The Drummond influence in the British railway scene had yet to perish, for in Scotland, on the Glasgow & South Western Railway, Peter Drummond continued as that line's new CME, to which post he had recently been appointed after some 18 years as Locomotive Superintendent of the Highland Railway. He was certainly keeping the Drummond name alive.

Dugald Drummond produced 24 of these useful and popular little passenger tanks of class '171' in 1884 for the Caledonian Railway. Fifteen survived to be given LMS numbers. One, No. 15103, survived all the others by 11 years to 1944, so this photograph of No. 15104 must have been taken before 1933.   *Jarvis Collection*

An example of perpetuation. This 4-4-0T by Lambie, built in 1893, still shows many Drummond features; Perth, 14th April, 1933.   *R.G. Jarvis/MRT*

Chapter Ten

To the Highland Railway

We now need to step back in time, to 1890, when Dugald departed for Australia. This move provided a split in the brothers' partnership. They were never to work together again under the same roof, although much communication clearly passed between them, particularly when Peter had risen to the top.

When Dugald resigned the Caledonian Railway Locomotive Superintendent's position, that office was filled by Hugh Smellie, formerly the Locomotive Superintendent of the Glasgow & South Western Railway. It has been suggested that Dugald may well have pre-warned the CR Board as to his imminent resignation for, at the very same Board Meeting at which his letter of resignation was minuted, the appointment of Smellie as his successor was approved.

Hugh Smellie, however, only held office for a short while, as he died suddenly on the 19th April, 1891, just a few months after taking over. He was aged just 51. The Board acted swiftly to this sudden and totally unexpected loss and appointed the Assistant Locomotive Superintendent, John Lambie, to the vacant post.

Peter Drummond was by now an assistant works manager and, in the reshuffle that went on after Smellie's death was elevated to the deputy works manager's position. The family had recently moved to No. 399, Parliamentary Road, still conveniently near the works.

His competent handling of production matters at St Rollox clearly merited this rise. He was now in the enviable position of being a front runner for future promotion to the Locomotive Superintendent's job should he eventually rise to the works managership, but there was one little snag. This was that the CR Board seemed now to be selecting their replacement Superintendents from Running Department men, for Lambie had risen from that department to his assistant's position. However, he was 58, so Peter could see the possibility of taking over in some seven or eight years and settled down into his deputy manager's job to await events.

Smellie's few months in office had resulted in no new locomotives other than a final batch of Dugald Drummond 'Gourock Bogies' being ordered from the works. However, Lambie immediately saw to the completion of the 4-4-0s and launched into the design of a 4-4-0T before turning his efforts to a batch of six new 4-4-0s which, although based on the earlier Drummond designs, departed from features such as dome safety valves, these being replaced by valves over the firebox. He also provided a larger boiler working at a higher pressure of 160 psi. These Drummond derivatives appeared in 1894.

A further tank design appeared the year after, this being a batch of 0-4-4Ts. Then tragedy struck the Caledonian again on 1st February, 1895, when Lambie died after a short illness. Yet another shuffle in the top hierarchy was to take place and Peter, who was hoping to become Works Manager in this, sensed that the choice of successor could have a decisive effect upon his further advancement on the CR. Dugald had been back from Australia for some time now and was

The first British 4-6-0, the HR Jones Goods.   *John Scott-Morgan Collection*

A splendid view of Jones Goods 4-6-0 No. 114 at Luncarty with a lengthy mixed goods train.

running his small engineering business in Glasgow, but was already being canvassed for the LSWR post, so he really never was in contention as a possible new Superintendent. Had he been offered the CR job, and accepted it, this would also have precluded Peter's further advancement on that railway.

Having selected a man well-versed in running matters as was Lambie, the CR Board decided to follow suit for the next incumbent of the Locomotive Superintendent's post, and chose John Farquharson McIntosh who up to then had been the chief inspector in the Running Department. This was, in the event, a wise choice for McIntosh had worked his way up from fireman and driver, and thus knew the CR men and locomotives from the 'inside'. He had earned the respect of footplate crews and workmen alike by being one of them all along. Sympathy and understanding were his great virtues, and these also permeated through into his dealings with the workforce, which contrasted with the earlier abrasive and dictatorial manner of the Drummonds. He had left the footplate in 1876 following an accident as the result of which he suffered a maimed right arm and been transferred to the Running Department.

The new, popular, Locomotive Superintendent was 49 years old and clearly had many years of service ahead. Peter saw little prospect of achieving the top position on the CR following the Board's confirmation of the appointment of McIntosh after six months of probationary service. He accordingly began to cast his eyes elsewhere.

Peter Drummond's thoughts on Dugald's departure for Australia followed by the setting up of the Glasgow works before the opportunity of the LSWR Superintendency are not on record. However, he must have felt some degree of loss of a steady adviser tinged with relief that at last he could go his own way without Dugald watching all the time. In 1895, shortly after Dugald departed for Nine Elms, Peter had been promoted to Works Manager at St Rollox to replace Robert Urie who was following his old chief down to the LSWR.

Although Dugald could have asked Peter to come to Nine Elms as Works Manager, that would have precluded any chance of his further elevation to Locomotive Superintendent. This raises the speculation that Dugald knew that Peter was fully capable of running his own show and deliberately did not reactivate the old partnership. Also, the imposition of a double dose of Drummonds on the LSWR may well have raised some sparks!

The opportunity to advance further came within that year, as the Highland Railway's Locomotive Superintendent, David Jones, had to resign following injuries received from a bad accident whilst testing a new engine. Jones had been in that position since Stroudley had departed for the LB&SCR, and a very successful and popular Superintendent at that. His penultimate design was the famous Jones Goods 4-6-0, the first locomotive to employ that wheel arrangement in the UK.

In all, Jones had been at Lochgorm for 41 years and, as we have seen in Part One, had worked briefly with Dugald all those years ago under Stroudley. The HR Directors cast around for a suitable replacement and, out of the 33 applications for the job, selected Peter. The official offer came on 7th October, 1896. The reputation of the Drummond competence clearly had something to do with their choice, and Peter certainly had managed matters on the CR well enough to make his mark. The opportunity for his advancement to the ultimate position was taken and, in November, he moved himself and the family to Inverness and the HR, living in a rented house, Achmonie, in Victoria Terrace, which was to be their home for the duration of his Superintendency there.

The Drummond influence was thus to return to Lochgorm works for the next 16 years. The works were still small and it was a close-knit workforce, many of whom had 30 or more years of service. The return of a Drummond to Inverness may well have produced some apprehensive reactions from the longer-serving hands there.

Peter was radically to change the outline and appearance of the 4-4-0 on the HR. In keeping with Dugald's designs for this type, he adopted inside cylinders. Out went the Jones style of cab and chimney and in came Drummond features. The safety valves also appeared on the dome. Other ideas copied, or suggested, from his elder brother were introduced as time went on as we shall see.

As regards his impact on the staff at Lochgorm works, where he soon became known as 'PD', Peter was very similar in attitude to that of Dugald, dictatorial and strict in his dealings with those under him. The Drummond attitudes had clearly rubbed off onto him in all those impressionable years when Dugald held sway over him. However, he never seemed to gain such a reputation as that of his elder brother.

Matters at the small cramped Lochgorm works were far from ideal for Peter's liking. Compared to his previous position at St Rollox, the HR works required a complete overhaul to restore some degree of efficiency to the output of the premises. He accordingly started making plans for the reorganization of the shops, in which he was to modernise where possible the older machines and tools.

At the ARLE summer meeting of 1897, held at the Manor House Hotel, Leamington Spa, Peter was elected to membership of this body. A subject under discussion at this meeting was that of boiler explosions, a rare but often catastrophic event. Bowman Malcolm of the Belfast & Northern Counties Railway was present and gave details of a recent such happening on that line which, it was thought, had occurred due to some faulty boiler/firebox stays. Much discussion revolved around how to adequately guard against this, with Harry Pollitt of the Great Central contributing a lucid discussion of the problem.

The HR had several features unique to its arrangement and location. The former being that much of the main lines were single track, so each locomotive required the fitting of tablet catching equipment, yet one more gadget to be maintained. The latter feature of location meant that in the winter there was always the need to keep lines open during heavy falls of snow. A good proportion of routes were at altitudes of up to nearly 1,500 feet, where snowfalls were considerably heavier than those at lower altitudes.

For instance, the main line from Perth to Inverness climbed to 1,484 feet above sea level at Druimuachdar and, at one time, was the highest main line in the British Isles. Peter designed an improved form of snow plough for use over the network, which materially helped in keeping lines open more efficiently. The HR used up to three locomotives coupled together with this plough on the front one, to charge deep drifts which tended to build up in cuttings, a practice which sometimes failed due to the sheer volume of packed snow to be shifted. There were some periods when lines were closed for days on end and trains were trapped, perhaps one of the most spectacular being a fish special which was snowed up and abandoned. Completely buried for 10 days, when finally dug out the contents were found to be in perfect condition and delivered to their intended destination!

Peter started his time at Inverness on motive power matters cautiously, in that his first three locomotive designs were based on those of others, the first two being derived from his brother Dugald and the third from an earlier study by his predecessor on the HR, Jones, the design of which was close to being completed for the consideration of the Traffic Department and, subsequently, the Board. The chief draughtsman at Lochgorm was a David Hendrie, who had served under Jones for many years and was well-versed in the needs of the HR motive power and stock. Peter wisely let Hendrie lead the small team with the minimum of change and merely oversaw the early deliberations whilst sizing up the areas of this last Jones design which needed attention. As he settled into his first Superintendent's position, brother Dugald was clearly indicating that certain of his current designs could, with appropriate modifications, be suitable. From the study of Peter's first two designs, a 4-4-0 and an 0-6-0, a clear link with Dugald's similar types on the LSWR is to be seen, so quite probably technical details and general arrangement drawings had been supplied from Nine Elms.

However, one of Peter's first exercises was to get the small team to design some third class and composite bogie coaches for main line services. The former were 48 feet long and had seven compartments, with the latter slightly shorter having two first class and four third class compartments. Lavatories were

One of the five 'Yankee Tanks' built by Dübs in 1891 for the Uruguay Eastern Railway but never exported, being eventually bought by the HR. LMS No. 15013 is seen at Dingwall on 2nd August, 1933.   *R.G. Jarvis/MRT*

provided in both types. The appearance of these early bogie coaches began the introduction of such stock on a much wider scale than hitherto. He also oversaw the completion of the switch from oil to gas lighting for passenger stock and saw to it that steam heating was to become the norm.

When the new carriages appeared their livery was changed from the green with yellow lining and lettering to one in which the upper panels were painted white. Quite often, a new Locomotive Superintendent would stamp his particular livery choice on the stock as an indication of his preferences. However, later in 1903 a decision was made to revert to an all-green livery, quite possibly on the grounds of economy.

The HR had, in 1885, pioneered the use of Pullman cars on the Scottish railways, having two first class sleeping cars built at the Midland Railway Derby works. Each accommodated 16 passengers in upper and lower berths. The main use was on overnight trains between Inverness and Perth. As time went on, the number of passengers requiring sleeping accommodation fell away until, in 1907, it was decided to withdraw the Pullmans from service and Peter was ordered to design replacements which could double up as a sleeping car and conventional carriage. The result was a coach having four single-berth first class sleeping compartments divided by an attendant's compartment from four third class compartments, each seating eight and one with a seat on one side, seating four. These vehicles were built by Hurst, Nelson & Co. of Motherwell and proved exceedingly useful, particularly where balance working was concerned on day trains. All survived into LMS days.

Peter's designs for carriage stock became virtually standard until Grouping, the only major refinements added after his departure being the appearance of electric lighting just after the end of World War I. His introduction of new heavy bogie stock also reinforced the arguments for larger, more powerful, passenger locomotive types.

Locomotive servicing and maintenance on the HR tended to be concentrated during the winter months when the services tapered off from the busy summer season. As late autumn approached stock awaiting attention would begin to build up outside Lochgorm works. So long as winter services were sparse this was a satisfactory way to arrange servicing schedules. But, as we shall see, this could not always be guaranteed.

As regards the works situation, the improvements began in the boiler shop by the installation of an air compressor and reservoir to supply pneumatic power to boring and tapping machines introduced by Peter to speed the construction and repair of boilers. On top of that major change, a complete rearrangement of the machine shop was carried out, in which the machines were positioned in four rows down its length, their drives being taken from a line shafting running down the centre of the shop.

In August 1897, after implementing his works reorganization and taking stock of the condition of some of the locomotives then operating, Peter reported to the Board that 17 examples were worn out and needed urgent replacements. He had already instigated some studies into a new 4-4-0 for passenger use and shortly after his report some provisional drawings were proffered. Seventeen replacements based on this design were then authorised.

Chapter Eleven

Peter at Lochgorm

Now he was firmly established on the HR, Peter began to assess what further locomotives were needed to augment the existing stock and, turning to Dugald's work proposed two initial types, firstly the 4-4-0, which we have seen was authorised, followed by an 0-6-0.

The classic inside-cylindered 4-4-0 was, for passenger and mixed-traffic use, virtually a Drummond trademark. The ease with which this type encountered sharply-curved track made it especially popular on the Scottish railways which abounded with plentiful curves in the mountains and glens of much of that country. So it was natural for Peter to bring out a 4-4-0 as his first offering for the HR.

The 'Ben' class of 4-4-0 followed closely the lines of Dugald's 'C8' for the LSWR, apart from the 6 ft diameter driving wheels specified by Peter (the 'C8' had 6 ft 7 in. drivers) and were intended for secondary passenger duties on the northernmost lines of the HR.

Twenty were, in fact, built between 1898 and 1906. The first eight, built by Dübs, had lever reverse, later changed to the steam reverse as per Drummond, to bring them into line with the final 12, nine of which were products of Lochgorm works. One of the first batch produced by Dübs, No. 2 *Ben Alder*, lingered on after the last withdrawal date of 1953 for some 13 years, being stored at Inverness, where it was less likely to attract the attention of those keen to eliminate steam altogether, for possible restoration and preservation. However, it failed to escape the net and was sadly cut up in 1966, before the preservation movement had got properly under way.

The 'Bens' never suffered from relegation in the way of Dugald's 'C8', in that they lasted much of their lives on the secondary duties for which they were built. It is interesting to note that the Dübs built examples cost £3,025 each, whereas the Lochgorm batch came out at £2,494 each. But, of course, Lochgorm did not need to take into consideration any profit. The livery of the new passenger locomotives was the early Drummond one of olive-green with black and double white lining.

As the new 4-4-0s appeared in traffic, some of the older stock was withdrawn for scrapping. In September 1898 the HR bade farewell to its final single-driver tender locomotive, 2-2-2 No. 32 *Cluny* which had been one of a class of 18, the remaining 17 having been rebuilt into 2-4-0s under Jones.

The last three examples of the 'Ben' were ordered from The North British Locomotive Company, into which Dübs had been merged, in 1906 and were costed at £3,450 each. Clearly some inflation was present over the eight years between the initial and final production examples.

With the assured success of the Ben 4-4-0 Peter turned his mind to an 0-6-0 which clearly took its styling, and much else, from Dugald's '700' class on the LSWR. On this design Peter adopted Dugald's water tube firebox, but notably these only appeared on the second (1902) batch of four out of the 12 produced,

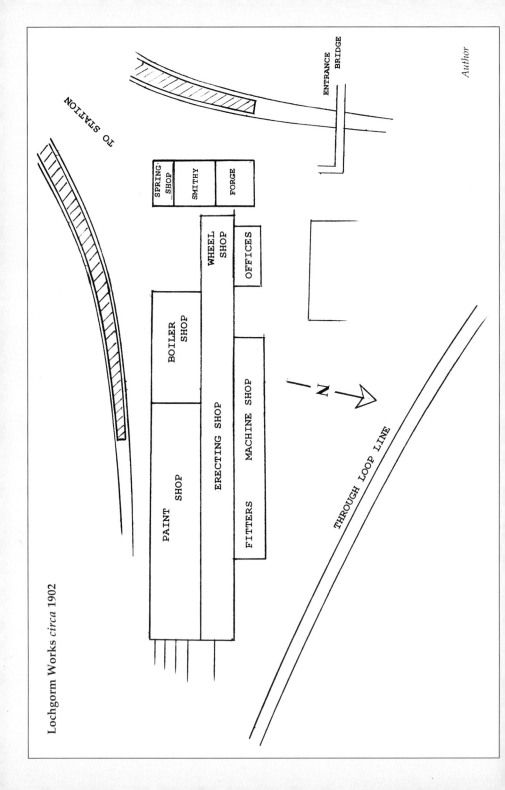

Lochgorm Works *circa* 1902

TO STATION

SPRING-SHOP

SMITHY

FORGE

WHEEL SHOP

OFFICES

BOILER SHOP

PAINT SHOP

ERECTING SHOP

MACHINE SHOP

FITTERS

N

ENTRANCE BRIDGE

THROUGH LOOP LINE

Author

The first of the 'Ben' class, No. 1 *Ben-y-Gloe*, Dübs & Co., 1898.

HR No. 5 *Ben Vrackie*. Compare this with Dugald's 'C8'. *John Scott-Morgan Collection*

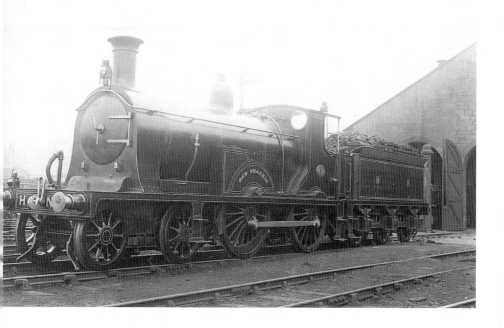

'Ben' class 4-4-0 No. 10 *Ben Slioch* in immaculate condition alonside Lochgorm works.

John Alsop Collection

and were to be the only application by Peter of this feature so widely used by Dugald. Other Drummond paraphernalia was omitted from this design, as it had been for the 'Ben'. One detects a slight drifting away from his elder brother's philosophy at about this time, after all, he was his own master and the influence was now firmly placed some few hundred miles away at Nine Elms. Dugald was only too willing to supply details of his current designs to Peter - plus suggestions as to the use of sundry other fads - but the remoteness of his sometimes overpowering personality certainly limited the pressure to follow the 'Drummond' way completely, although it was to be some years before this influence died away completely, as we shall see.

The 0-6-0s were authorised on 7th September, 1898, 15 being the initial number anticipated. The order was placed with Dübs who quoted £43,725 for the complete batch. This figure was a bit on the high side, thought some members of the Board. Lochgorm, with its limited production capacity, was already fully committed on the 4-4-0s and was not in a position to produce the 0-6-0s, so Peter was dispatched to Glasgow to see if any reduction in price could be negotiated. He returned with a reduced quote of £41,250 which appeared to satisfy the critics. However, very soon after, this order was to be modified yet again, as will be seen.

These 0-6-0s proved useful engines on all secondary goods work and, although officially known as class 'K', they soon acquired the nickname 'Barneys'. This is thought to have been connected to either the visit of Barnum and Bailey's circus to Scotland in 1900 or a driver named Barney who made a spectacular braking application on one of the locomotives when hauling a loose-coupled goods train. This braking caught the guard unawares and resulted in dozens of wagons being spread over the track as they tried to continue their journey at speed.

Of these 0-6-0s, No. 135, of the first Dübs batch, achieved notoriety behind the scenes for the trout that lived in the tender tank for some five years. It had apparently been caught in the Mill Burn at Inverness in 1909, but exactly how it got into the tank remains a mystery. However, once the shed staff knew of it's location, it was adopted as a 'mascot', being regularly fed by cleaners and crews alike. When the locomotive was in the shops for repairs special provision was made to find it an alternative home. It disappeared in old age having been well-travelled after the years of living in its mobile home. Had the feed-water heating been installed, this habitat would not have been possible and would have resulted in trout cooked to a turn!

Despite earlier comments on the social acceptability of the Drummonds in Inverness (re Jones' daughter's criticism mentioned in Chapter One) Peter's family clearly fitted in well during his Superintendency on the HR, for in 1905 his eldest daughter, Jeanie, married Dr Peter Mckellar Dewar, a medical practitioner. The wedding took place on 7th June at St Stephen's Church in Inverness. This happy family event was to be marred by the death of her cousin, Walter, on 7th July.

Whereas Dugald had waited until 1905 before bringing out a 4-6-0 design for passenger work, Peter entered the fray on the HR with the 'Castle' class 4-6-0 in 1900. Admittedly he had the almost complete design study initiated by Jones,

Peter Drummond in 1902.   *Railway Magazine*

'K' class or 'Barney' 0-6-0 No. 134 was the first in the class and was delivered by Dübs in 1900, remaining in service until 1949. *John Alsop Collection*

'Barney' class 0-6-0 No. 21 in 1911 with a lengthy passenger train at Muir of Ord, the junction for Fortrose.

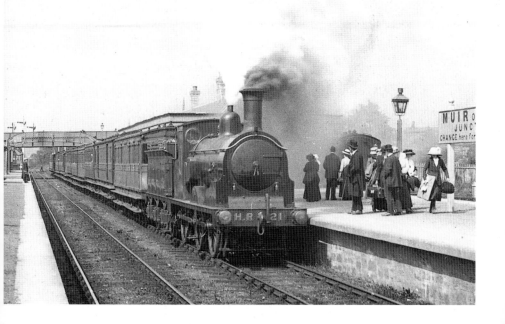

'Castle' class 4-6-0 No. 148 *Cawdor Castle* at Perth. This locomotive was delivered by Dübs in July 1902 and was taken out of service in April 1937.   *John Alsop Collection*

'Castle' class No. 58 *Darnaway Castle* at Perth in 1923. The 'Castle' class was delivered in three batches under three different Locomotive Superintendents, Peter Drummond, Frederick Smith and finally Christopher Cumming. Each batch had detail differences. No. 58 was one of the Cumming batch of 'Castles', which were delivered by North British of Glasgow in 1917. This third batch of locomotives had 6 ft driving wheels in place of the 5 ft 9 in. wheels used on the two earlier batches.

mentioned in the previous Chapter, to work on. It is abundantly clear that he made very few changes to that design, for the resulting locomotive certainly did not have a 'Drummond' look. Clearly, Peter had taken note of the considerable success of the 'Jones Goods' design which, at the time of its introduction, had been claimed as the most powerful locomotive in Britain with its tractive effort of 24,555 lb. and was the catalyst for this new passenger type. Seeing that it was basically the earlier 4-6-0 with larger (5 ft 9 in. as against 5 ft 3 in.) wheels, he had wisely decided that it would be foolish to start with a clean sheet.

The changes he made to Jones' design were limited to the valves and big ends, the former being changed from piston valves to balanced slide valves and the latter to the standard Drummond preference for the marine type. Piston valves were still a relatively new feature and the Drummond philosophy was to wait until all the bugs had been ironed out by others before adopting them. A steam reverser was also incorporated on all those produced whilst Peter was at Inverness. The class totalled 12 at the end of Peter's incumbency and, such was their usefulness, a further seven appeared under his successors, Smith (4) and Cumming (3) after he had left for the Glasgow & South Western Railway. The final three under Cumming differed in that they had screw reversing plus driving wheels of 6 ft in diameter.

All the 'Castles' were built by Dübs (1900-02) and North British (1910-17). The negotiations that led to the first batch were somewhat unorthodox. There was the order placed with Dübs for 15 0-6-0s at £41,250. This was renegotiated in 1900 to become an order for six 0-6-0s and six 4-6-0s, as the first 0-6-0s were being delivered. Peter wished to change the design of the 0-6-0 to incorporate firebox cross water tubes (Dugald had clearly suggested he try this feature) and the drawings would take time. In order to keep some form of continuity with deliveries the follow-on batch of 0-6-0s were to be transferred to a new order and were substituted by the first 4-6-0s. The total cost of this first amended order was unchanged at £41,250. On that basis the 4-6-0s worked out at £4,125 each. This neat piece of juggling by Peter clearly helped the Board's worries about revenue cash-flows with many of the new locomotives then being charged to the revenue accounts.

In passing, it is worth noting that the NBL-built 'Castles' cost £3,820 each in 1910-11. Probably this reduction was assisted by a forthcoming order from France. This class was notable for the fact that a batch of 50 were supplied to the French State Railways (ETAT) in 1911 to fulfil an urgent need for passenger locomotives in that country. These were identical to the early HR locomotives except that they were fitted with air brakes. This export order must have given Peter considerable satisfaction and boosted his status to the HR Board. Fifty locomotives was a sizeable order for North British at a time when that company, an amalgamation of Dübs, Nielson's and Sharp, Stewart, was establishing itself as a major supplier to the World railway market.

The French order was placed in January 1911 and 12 weeks after that, the first five were being shipped to France, the balance being supplied at five per week to completion. By 1938, they had all been withdrawn and scrapping was under way, but three survived to be resurrected in 1941 and were employed on hauling workmen's trains around Evreux. These were not the only British

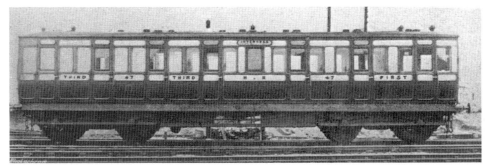

Highland Railway bogie corridor composite carriage built under Peter Drummond.
Railway Magazine

New stock under construction in the carriage works at Inverness.   *Railway Magazine*

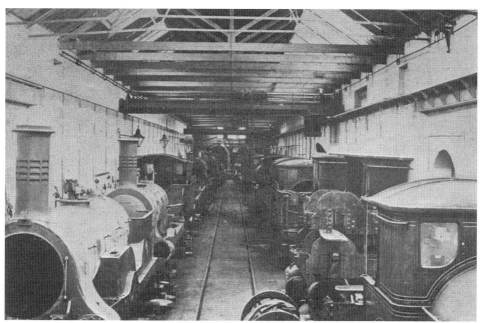

The interior of Lochgorm works erecting shop. *Railway Magazine*

The machine shop, Lochgorm works. *Railway Magazine*

'V' class or 'Scrap Tank' 0-6-0 No. 22 at Inverness. It was one of three powerful shunting engines built from parts salvaged from earlier withdrawn locomotives in 1903 and 1904.

John Alsop Collection

One of the three 'Scrap Tanks' No. 16382 in LMS days, shunting at Perth *c.*1929.

R.G. Jarvis/MRT

locomotives to be found operating in occupied France, for a batch of LMS class '2F' 0-6-0Ts had been left behind in 1940 by the BEF and were pressed into service around occupied Northern France.

Out of the 72 locomotives of Peter's designs, only 19 emerged from Lochgorm works, the remainder being contracted out to the private builders. The limited capacity of the works was almost completely taken up with the normal rebuilding and servicing tasks on the fleet of around 160-170 locomotives. The biggest production batch of any type was four in any one year.

Of the 19 home-produced locomotives, two types were tanks, consisting of three 0-6-0Ts and four 0-4-4Ts. The remainder were the 12 'Bens' already mentioned.

The 0-6-0Ts came from the discussion that ensued after Peter had prepared a report for the Locomotive Committee on the condition of the stock. In the paragraphs covering the problems with some rebuilt 2-4-0s which had been given new boilers by Jones, he emphasised that the frame cracking being experienced by some was directly attributable to the increased boiler weight. He then suggested that three of these 2-4-0s could provide many useful parts for a batch of 0-6-0 shunting tanks. At first this suggestion was glossed over, but at a subsequent meeting this suggestion was raised again and a recommendation made to go ahead with the proposal.

The parts for the subsequent design came from Barclay, Jones and Drummond designs, many of which were lying around or in store. The tanks, of class 'V', were specifically for shunting duties and, owing to the employment of parts salvaged from some obsolete 2-4-0s, were outside cylindered. The boilers were recovered from the 2-4-0s and the wheels of 5 ft 2½ inches were from a similar source. That diameter was unusually large for a shunting locomotive but needs must when finance is short. So many parts were used from withdrawn types that, in later years, these useful little engines were dubbed 'Scrap Tanks'. Two were based at Inverness and the other at Perth. Costed at £1,650 each, which was charged to revenue, they proved a useful addition to the HR stock, and were rather attractive little locomotives.

Following this 0-6-0T came a batch of four class 'W' 0-4-4Ts for light passenger work on branch lines. Unmistakeably Drummond in layout, these neat little engines all passed into LMS ownership at Grouping with two surviving into the Nationalisation era. Of these two No. 55053 lasted until 1957 on the Dornoch branch. This might have survived until the closure of that branch in 1960 but suffered a broken crank axle in 1957 and was withdrawn and scrapped. It most certainly was the last of Peter Drummond's designs for the HR to remain working in revenue service.

Before the final, for the HR, tank locomotive, in 1908 Peter ordered a redesign of the 'Ben' 4-4-0. This type, to be known as class 'U', or the 'New Ben', was essentially a large-boilered derivative of the 'Ben'. North British got the order for the complete class of six examples. The 'New Ben' was significant in that it was the first Peter Drummond design to employ safety valves over the firebox, rather than the normal Drummond dome position. But, by this time Dugald had brought out his first 4-6-0s with safety valves in the more conventional location. Yet another small departure from the Drummond tradition had emerged.

'W' class 0-4-4T No. 25 *Strathpeffer* was built in March 1905. The 'W' class was the last to be built at Lochgorm works.   *John Alsop Collection*

No. 55053 is in immaculate condition having just been outshopped at St Rollox works on 2nd July, 1955. It is ready to return north to resume work on the Dornoch branch. This 'W' class locomotive was built as No. 45 in December 1905. When it was withdrawn in January 1957 it was the last remaining example of a Highland Railway locomotive in service.   *W.S. Sellar*

Never as popular as the earlier 'Ben' class, the 'New Ben' was, as a class all withdrawn by 1937, despite having been superheated by the LMS between 1923-27. Apparently, the superheating had little effect upon their coal consumption, so one is tempted to believe that the valve travel was a bit on the sparse side resulting in a relatively choked exhaust and attendant back-pressure. However, by the mid-1930s the Stanier 'Black Five' was beginning to appear over the LMS and displacing sundry other types more capable than the small classes on some of the Scottish lines.

The final offering from Peter's drawing board for the HR was a large 0-6-4T of class 'X' to be used on banking duties. However, the Traffic Department had other ideas and these tanks were to be found on more general duties on the main lines, including both passenger and goods work. Four were built by North British in 1909 and clearly the main line duties were so satisfactory that a further four appeared, also from North British, between 1910 and 1912, making the class total eight. The cylinders, motion and wheels were very similar to the earlier 0-6-0 'Drummond Goods', and the rear bogie was the same as that used on the 'Castle' class.

Amongst his own designs for the HR, Peter did not neglect rebuilding exercises where he saw that they could extend or improve the useful life of locomotives already in service when he arrived. A case in point is that of the 4-4-0Ts, or 'Yankee Tanks', which had been purchased from Dübs & Co. following economic problems of the Uruguay Eastern Railway which had ordered but been unable to take delivery of a batch of five. These locomotives had been in service on branch work since 1892-3 and one, No. 102, was brought into Lochgorm works in 1906 to be rebuilt with a larger boiler, increased tank capacity, and Drummond boiler mountings. This particular example, out of the two given such treatment, subsequently ran over 750,000 miles before scrapping by the LMS in 1934. This gives an idea as to the excellence of the output available at Lochgorm.

David Hendrie, who had been Jones' chief draughtsman, stayed on with Peter for some time before resigning, being replaced by Robert Collie after a few years. In turn Collie, in 1903, was replaced by David Smith who proved a dynamic and very competent assistant.

For a small design centre, a surprising number of project studies emanated under Peter Drummond in his time on the HR, starting as early as 1899 when initial sketches of an enlarged 'Ben' appeared. This had a bigger boiler and longer wheelbase and was clearly to be the catalyst for the later 'New Ben'.

The 4-4-0 theme was further developed in 1901 by a further enlargement of the 1899 study. This had a remarkable similarity to Dugald's last design for the LSWR, the 'D15'. However, much could have been different in the engineering sense, as the Drummond styling would have been the feature of note on the line diagram.

One scheme of particular interest was that for an 0-8-0 in 1902. This was some years before Dugald entered into studies for such an arrangement on the LSWR. Whether this study of Peter's influenced Dugald in those later years is not known, but could be possible. *Tables One* and *Two* summarise what has been unearthed about these project studies, *Table One* covering the tank and tender types, including the 0-8-0, and *Table Two* concentrating on the close similarities

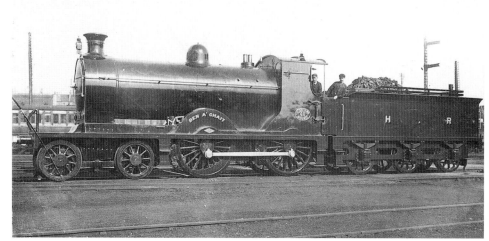

'New Ben' class 4-4-0 No. 68 *Ben a'Chait*. These locomotives had larger boilers than those on Drummond's earlier HR 4-4-0s.   *John Alsop Collection*

'New Ben' class 4-4-0 No. 60 *Ben Breac Mhor*. Notice that this was one of the two engines of this class which was fitted with a Westinghouse brake.   *John Alsop Collection*

of Peter's 1901 4-4-0 with Dugald's 'D15' and Peter's class '131' of 1912 and 1913 respectively. The tanks on *Table One* are both 0-4-4Ts and clearly the second later, and larger, variant was based on Dugald's very successful 'M7', then in quantity production for the LSWR.

A comparison between the 0-8-0s designed by the brothers is to be found in *Table Three*. A further 0-8-0 design, with a larger boiler and shorter wheelbase, was sketched but came to naught, but no details of this iteration have come to light.

In between the two 0-4-4Ts came a 4-6-0 notable for having a side-window cab and a large 4,400 gallon six-wheel tender, of which no other details have been found.

In early 1903 Peter had drawn to his notice the potential of the internal combustion engine for railway work. It was appearing on the streets as the fledgling motor industry began producing even better motorcars, lorries and buses. Also, at this time Dugald was beginning to design his steam rail motors and, clearly, had communicated some details to Peter. However, Peter's first foray into railcars consisted of a submission to the Locomotive Committee of 'a drawing and an estimate for a Petrol Electric self-contained car for light railways from the Wolseley Tool and Motor Car Co., Birmingham, which was examined'. Not surprisingly, this proposal got no further, but Peter was not to be dismayed and ordered the drawing office to prepare a design for a steam railcar based, it seems, on Dugald's 'H13' rail motor of 1905.

Peter clearly watched events in England and, seeing the limited performance of these low-powered units over the relatively level branches involved, quietly put his designs on one side.

By 1905 Dugald was bringing out his four-cylindered 4-6-0s, so Peter had some brief studies done into the layout and radical change in cylinder numbers. It too was side-lined.

Another 4-6-0 was schemed at Inverness in 1907, this being a mixed traffic type having 5 ft driving wheels. However, the existing fleet of 'Jones Goods' and 'Castles' was proving adequate and no further 4-6-0s could, at the time, be countenanced. This project is compared to the 'Castle' in *Table Four*.

There were sundry other studies carried out, but no sketches survive. It is known that 4-4-2 and further 4-6-0 designs were looked into briefly, both intended for passenger uses. The Atlantic was a clear sign that Peter intended to go his own way, for we have seen that Dugald was highly critical of this wheel arrangement and would have nothing to do with it.

Whilst the fleet on the HR was adequate for the normal seasonal traffic on that line, with servicing decided by the demands on the locomotive stock, any disruption to this would upset matters. But so long as there was no hint of war, the Home Fleet was based in the southern ports of Britain. Should hostilities cause the Fleet to be based at Scapa Flow, the logistics of keeping it supplied throughout the year would fall upon the HR and result in demands for motive power beyond its capability at some times. This, in fact, did happen in World War I, but by then Peter was elsewhere.

So, Peter was not idle in between times of the design and production of the HR types attributed to him. Some of the project studies were influenced by

Table One

Highland Railway Project Studies

Type	4-4-0	4-4-0	0-4-4T	0-8-0	0-4-4T	4-6-0
Year	1899	1901	1902	1902	1904	1907
Cylinders	18½ in. x 26 in.	19 in. x 26 in.	17 in. x 24 in.	20 in. x 26 in.	18 in. x 26 in.	18½ in. x 26 in.
Boiler Diameter	4 ft 9 in.	5 ft 0 in.	4 ft 3¼ in.	5 ft 3 in.	4 ft 6¾ in.	4 ft 6¾ in.
Boiler Pitch	7 ft 9 in.	8 ft 6 in.	7 ft 3 in.	8 ft 0 in.	7 ft 6 in.	7 ft 10 in.
Heating Area						
Tubes	1,280	1,390	979	1,995	1,061	1,433
Firebox	125	155	106	155	117	112
Crosstubes	-	215	-	180	-	-
Total	1,405	1,760	1,085	2,330	1,178	1,545
Grate Area	25.0	27.0	18.0	27.0	20.4	21.5
Pressure (psi)	175	175	175	175	175	180
Tractive effort (lb.)	18,384	17,899	17,195	27,140	18,160	22,032
Bogie wheels	3 ft 6 in.	3 ft 6 in.	3 ft 6 in.	-	3 ft 6 in.	3 ft 3 in.
Coupled wheels	6 ft 0 in.	6 ft 6 in.	5 ft 0 in.	5 ft 0 in.	5 ft 9 in.	5 ft 0 in.
Coupled wheelbase	9 ft 6 in.	10 ft 0 in.	-	19 ft 0 in.	-	11 ft 7 in.
For tank locomotives						
Water capacity (gallons)			1,200		1,600	
Coal (tons)			1¾		2	

Notes: There were sundry other design studies done at Lochgorm, for example a 4-4-2 and other 4-6-0s, but so little information is available, they have been omitted from this table.

All those listed above were two-cylinder designs.
It is of interest to note that Peter's design for an 0-8-0 predates Dugald's 0-8-0 by some five years. There was, apparently a further iteration on this HR project with a larger boiler and shorter wheelbase, but no further data is available. For a comparison of these 0-8-0s, see *Table Three.*
For a comparison of the 4-6-0 above and the 'Castle', see *Table Four.*

Table Two

The Large 4-4-0s compared to the 'D15'

	HR Project	'D15'	G&SWR class '131'
Year	1901	1912	1915
Cylinders	19 in. x 26 in.	19½ in. x 26 in.	19½ in. x 26 in.
Boiler diameter	5 ft 0 in.	4 ft 9½ in.	5 ft 0 in.
Boiler pitch	8 ft 6 in.	8 ft 9 in.	8 ft 6 in.
Heating area			
Tubes	1,390	1,406	1,680
Firebox	155	148	148
Crosstubes	215	170	-
Total	1,760	1,724	1,828
Grate area	27.0	27.0	27.5
Pressure (psi)	175	200	180
Tractive effort (lb)	17,899	21,274	21,009
Bogie wheels	3 ft 6 in.	3 ft 7 in.	3 ft 6 in.
Coupled wheels	6 ft 6 in.	6 ft 7 in.	6 ft 0 in.
Coupled wheelbase	10 ft 0 in.	10 ft 0 in.	10 ft 0 in.

The HR project was strangely prophetic of the 'D15'. The similarities in dimensions, heating areas and coupled wheels lead one to wonder if Dugald had the 'D15' in his sights much earlier on. Or did he take Peter's project study as a starting point? The boiler dimensions for the class '131' are a calculated guess.

'X' class 0-6-4T No. 68, the last class to be introduced by Peter Drummond on the Highland.
John Alsop Collection

No. 39 was the first of the class, it is seen here at Ballinluig on 18th September, 1912 with the Aberfeldy branch train.

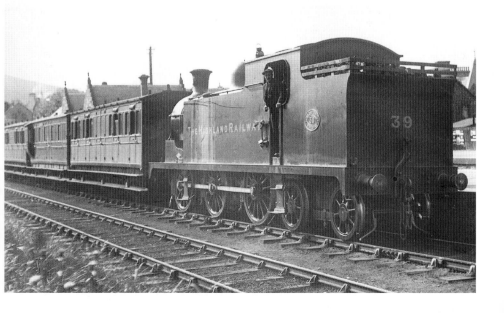

Table Three

Comparison of Peter and Dugald 0-8-0 Studies

	Peter (HR)	Dugald (LSWR)
Year	1902	1907
Cyls (diameter and stroke)	20 in. x 26 in. (2 inside)	16½ in. x 26 in. (4)
Valve gear	Stephenson*	Walschaert's
Boiler diameter	5 ft 3 in.	5 ft 6 in.
Boiler length	13 ft 9 in.	13 ft 9 in.
Boiler pitch	8 ft 0 in.	9 ft 0 in.
Heating areas (sq.ft)		
Tubes	1,995	2,120
Firebox	155	160
Crosstubes	180	357
Total	2,330	2,727
Grate area (sq. ft)	27.0	31.5
Pressure (psi)	175	175
Tractive Effort (lb)	27,140	36,307
Wheel diameter	4 ft 9 in. †	4 ft 10 in.
Wheelbase	19 ft 0 in.	17 ft 6 in.

* Balanced slide valves located beneath cylinders.
† Driving axle wheels flangeless.

Table Four

The mixed traffic 4-6-0 project compared to the 'Castle'

	1907 project	Castle
Cyls (diameter and stroke)	18¼ in. x 26 in.	19½ in. x 26 in.
Boiler diameter	4 ft 6¼ in.	5 ft 0 in.
Boiler length	12 ft 9 in.	14 ft 4½ in.
Boiler pitch	7 ft 10 in.	8 ft 2 in.
Heating areas (sq.ft)		
Tubes	1,433	1,916
Firebox	112	134
Total	1,545	2,050
Grate area (sq.ft)	21.5	26.5
Pressure (psi)	180	180
Tractive Effort (lb.)	22,032	21,922
Bogie wheels	3 ft 3 in.	3 ft 3 in.
Driving wheels	5 ft 0 in.	5 ft 9 in.
Coupled Wheelbase	11 ft 7 in.#	14 ft 3 in.

\# Driving axle wheels flangeless.

Quite possibly this project could have been for the Kyle line, with the short wheelbase and flangeless middle driving wheels. However, the shortage of funding and limited use effectively put an end to this interesting study. The Jones Goods were still very much active and coping well with freight work elsewhere as well as some passenger traffic.

liaison with his brother on the LSWR, yet we find some studies sufficiently independent to indicate that he was capable of going his own way. However, as we shall see in the next Chapter covering the Glasgow & South Western Railway, this way was not always to result in sparkling performance or reliability.

Dugald died in 1912. That year also brought about a change of job for Peter, for the G&SWR Locomotive Superintendent, James Manson, retired in 1912 and the Directors cast around for a suitable replacement. Peter's performance at Inverness was adequate enough for him to be selected for the position at the Kilmarnock works of the G&SWR. He had largely revamped the locomotive stock of the HR, bringing the fleet up to date and placing it in a good position to cope with the increasing traffic demands. And so he returned to the part of Scotland familiar to him from his earlier days and began to re-equip the G&SWR with new designs which, we will see, were of varying abilities. The Drummond abrasiveness was to be imbued upon yet another motive power production centre, although we shall see that this characteristic was to be somewhat modified in a few years.

To succeed Peter at Inverness came Frederick Smith, who had been Works Manager at Lochgorm since 1903. His term of office was to be overshadowed by the debacle over his 'River' class 4-6-0s, but that story is not appropriate in this context. Smith did, however, start off in style with a further batch of four 'Castle' class 4-6-0s which only differed from Peter's design by having extended smokeboxes and deflector chimneys.

A splendid view of Inverness shed in 1913. The locomotives on vew include two of the three 'Scrap Tanks', Jones Goods Nos. 105 and 113, 4-4-0 No. 119 *Loch Insch*, on the extreme left an unidentified 'Castle' class 4-6-0, as well as a fully loaded tender belonging to Drummond 'Barney' class 0-6-0 No. 20.

G&SWR 4-4-0 No. 98. Before Peter Drummond took office on the G&SWR, the express duties were undertaken by the graceful Manson 4-4-0s such as this one at Carlisle in 1900.

R.S.Carpenter Collection

Chapter Twelve

Peter on the G&SWR

The area covered by the Glasgow & South Western Railway was broadly inside the area to the west of the line connecting Glasgow and Carlisle. Within this area could be found major towns such as Kilmarnock, Ayr, Dumfries and Stranraer, all served from the St Enoch terminus in Glasgow. Much of the area south-west of Glasgow was predominately agricultural with moderate concentrations of industry, both of which provided a steady flow of traffic to the railway. Much commuter traffic flowed in and out of the populated areas and the line down to Carlisle provided a through route for joint Anglo-Scottish services. It was a busy, compact, railway, a key player in the economy of the Lowlands of Scotland.

Kilmarnock works was, like Lochgorm, a small concern, with much reliance on outside contractors for new builds, being mainly a repair and rebuild facility. Peter settled in with Mary at Belmont, Grange Terrace in Kilmarnock in 1912, to begin what was to be his final post. He had been in office for less than a year when the news of Dugald's accident, severe medical treatment and subsequent death came as a shock to him.

The salary commanded by Peter was £1,100, not much compared to Dugald's £5,000, but still, for the day, more than adequate to provide a comfortable life for him and his family. In present-day terms this £1,100 represents over £100,000.

In earlier Chapters we have seen that Peter's time on the HR had produced a mixed and on the whole satisfactory batch of locomotive designs, based mainly on types established by Jones or brother Dugald. He was hardly an accomplished innovator, but his choice of concepts, bolstered by support from Nine Elms, certainly were engineered in the true Drummond fashion - solidly. This ensured that, even when following others schemes the stock that resulted were satisfactory performers, despite being embellished with many of the design features so beloved of brother Dugald. The reliability on the HR, at least, seemed tolerably acceptable. He never fully adopted the full Dugald treatment after dutifully trying out various doubtful innovations, for example firebox cross water tubes - these were only to appear on one batch of the HR 0-6-0 and were not perpetuated, being discarded when fresh designs were being schemed. Some of the Drummond fads such as steam reversers (usually between the frames and thus largely inaccessible for maintenance), 'Steam Driers' as Dugald persisted in calling his low degree superheating gadget, feed-water heating apparatus in the tender plus duplex feed-water pumps, lingered on for some time and were taken with him to the G&SWR.

There was one feature of the G&SWR locomotive stock which Peter did deal with early on in his time at Kilmarnock. This was to modify the whole fleet so that fusible plugs were fitted to the fireboxes. Surprisingly, this vital safety feature had, up to then, never been incorporated on that railway. All the previous Locomotive Superintendents had, for some reason, omitted to ensure their inclusion.

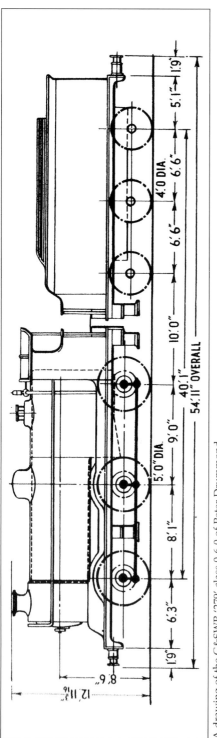

A drawing of the G&SWR '279' class 0-6-0 of Peter Drummond.

An official photograph of '279' class 0-6-0 No. 300.

John Alsop Collection

Noticeably, the initial G&SWR locomotives to emanate from Peter were not all that successful. Whether this has anything to do with Dugald no longer being available for consultation is not known, but the fall-off in performance certainly coincides with this time. The earlier HR designs were much better overall but, of course, he had had the capable assistance of a very competent chief draughtsman in David Smith on that railway for the last seven of his 15 years in office at Inverness. Peter must have had a high opinion of Smith, for he took him to Kilmarnock and installed him as chief draughtsman there.

Peter had arrived at Kilmarnock in 1912 and imposed his overbearing, rough, manner on the workforce. He had little but contempt for his predecessor, Manson, and showed his authority in repeated threats of instant dismissal to all who disobeyed his orders. He was not at all popular. Little has filtered through about his manner at Lochgorm but it does not seem to have been as bad as that imposed on the G&SWR. This attitude persisted until 1915, as did the production of troublesome locomotives. Then a transformation occurred, in that he simmered down, became quieter and was fair and wise in his dealings with the workforce. A new man indeed. After this, his locomotives became the reliable, economic, products that the railway expected. The change of manner meant that his design team could offer suggestions instead of not daring to do so for fear of instant dismissal.

As had Dugald, Peter took a considerable interest in the education of apprentices and the workforce, encouraging them to enrol in suitable spare or part-time courses available locally. He realised that a knowledgeable workforce would more likely give of their best both in the design and production tasks allotted them. The response to his encouragements in such matters was probably better in his final years of office once his temperament had moderated.

However, there was one matter which Peter instigated once settled into Kilmarnock which was to make all new locomotives left-hand drive. Up to then the G&SWR had been a right-hand drive line. This did not please the crews one bit.

The first locomotive Peter designed at Kilmarnock was a large 0-6-0, class '279'. Fifteen were built by North British in 1913. They were, at the time, the heaviest 0-6-0 ever built in Britain, turning the scales at 57¾ tons, plus a further 47 tons for the tender, and were put onto heavy goods work between Glasgow and Carlisle. The inside motion was Stephenson link which drove piston valve via rockers. Unfortunately this proved a retrograde feature in that this form of linkage was virtually guaranteed to produce a sluggish engine. This these lumbering 0-6-0s were from the outset, plus being notorious coal gobblers, with 90-100 lb. per mile the norm. Failures were all too frequent due to the excessive gadgetry - this reminds the author of a comment made by Sir William Stanier about Churchward instilling into his staff the need to minimise gadgets on locomotives, which was why Swindon designs were renowned for reliability and freedom from excessive maintenance tasks. There were also some cases of overheating associated with the introduction of marine type big ends, the first such application on the G&SWR, which required the application of vast quantities of lubricating oil to try and keep matters cool. Timekeeping on many of the tasks allotted these 'Pumpers', as the enginemen quickly dubbed them,

'131' class 4-4-0 No. 335 (formerly No. 135) pulls away from Monkton with a passenger train.

John Alsop Collection

A view of No. 335 on a passenger train near Troon.   *John Alsop Collection*

Peter Drummond's big 4-4-0: class '137' No. 330 is seen on a passenger train.

was almost impossible if a heavy load was involved. Matters were so serious that the crews sent a petition to Peter in which they demanded extra pay and bonus for dealing with the lubrication and firing of these troublesome locomotives. They clearly made a good case, for they got their demand in the sum of 6*d*. per trip from Carlisle to Glasgow or vice versa - providing that three-quarters of the trip was made without failure. With all the Drummond gadgets removed early on the 0-6-0s struggled on in minor duties for the LMS after Grouping, but were scrapped between 1930 and 1933.

With Dugald's final design for the LSWR, the 'D15' 4-4-0, in service and proving a powerful addition to the express fleet of that railway, it was natural for Peter to consider this for his first passenger 4-4-0 on the G&SWR, which appeared in 1913.

The class '131' that ensued, apart from smaller driving wheels and safety valves over the firebox, was unmistakeably the 'D15' in 'Scottish' guise. It even went as far as employing Walschaert's valve gear, a first for Peter, as had the 'D15'. They were also heavier than the 'D15' and in fact were the heaviest British 4-4-0 around at the time of their appearance. As with the 0-6-0s, they incorporated all the Drummond gadgetry. The feed pumps on both the 0-6-0s and 4-4-0s gave great trouble at first, the problem eventually being traced to poor casting manufacture which throttled performance due to bad passages. The feed pumps were removed as early as 1915, just two years after the batch of six 4-4-0s had been built by North British.

Six locomotives spread over the network of the G&SWR proved to be too few and their performance was not particularly sparkling. They were sluggish and proved to be poor hill climbers so Peter resolved to do something about this. Accordingly, in 1915, a further batch of six appeared, this time from Kilmarnock

An official photograph of '16' class 2-6-0 No. 403.   *John Alsop Collection*

'16' class 2-6-0 No. 55 at Dumfries.   *John Alsop Collection*

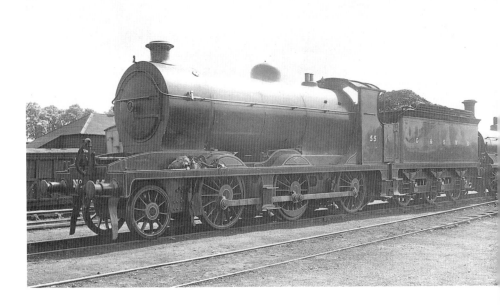

works, and had one major difference in that they were superheated. Unlike the earlier saturated batch, these later locomotives were free runners so one is led to speculate that Peter had made some alterations to the motion, but he had not followed Dugald's lead on the 'D15' and employed outside admission valves. Just plain superheating seems to be inadequate to produce such an about turn on free running. The saturated engines, save for one example, were progressively superheated between 1923-31 by the LMS, but all were scrapped by 1937.

By now, the British nation was fully engaged in World War I and the demand on the railway network was at a peak. Yet more goods locomotives were needed and an order was placed on Peter in November 1914 for an additional number.

The year 1915 brought a pleasant task for Peter. Some time previously, daughter Christina had met a George Alexander Burnett, the Rector of Montrose Academy. Despite his being on the other side of the country, the friendship deepened and on 14th July of that year they were married, with Christina conducted down the aisle of High Church, Kilmarnock by her father.

Turning back to his 0-6-0s, Peter had his team scheme a 'stretched' version which necessitated adding a pony truck in front of the leading drivers, producing the 2-6-0, or Mogul layout, which was given the class '16' designation. Superheated from the start, the 11 examples were produced by North British and immediately put into service at Carlisle for the main line goods services up into Scotland. They proved to be free runners, excellent on hills and economic on coal. Fifty loaded wagons were no trouble to these new examples and was the standard load to be found behind these excellent freight locomotives. A complete change from the saturated and sluggish 0-6-0s.

The appearance of locomotives having an acceptable performance coincided with the dramatic change in Peter's personality mentioned earlier. It was as though the final veil had been lifted with the realisation that Dugald, with his aggressive and stubborn views, was no longer in the background to proffer his ideas on the way Peter should go. Teamwork, in its proper sense, could be practised. However, for the time being, Peter still insisted on incorporating the gadgets, so inured was he to their appearance that nothing could persuade him to discontinue them.

As with Dugald, Peter's attendance at the ARLE meetings was sparse and he was never on record as having taken part in the proceedings. Quite probably, big brother's negative views on the usefulness of the association had a bearing on this. In any case, the minutes are sketchy in some areas and whilst Peter may have attended the occasional Scottish venue whilst Dugald was about, his contributions worthy of note were clearly minimal.

The G&SWR had but a few tank engines, with all these restricted to local passenger or shunting tasks. However, for some of the Ayrshire coalfield tasks, Peter made a decision that over the limited distances involved a large tank engine could be of considerable use. He designed an 0-6-2T version of his HR 0-6-4T by simply replacing the rear bogie with a pair of radial wheels and shortening the bunker, which was designated class '45'. As much of the work involved long periods of shunting and relatively short hauls, superheaters were not fitted.

An official photograph of '45' class 0-6-2T No. 45.   *John Alsop Collection*

An official photograph of '1' class 0-6-2T No. 1.   *John Alsop Collection*

''5' class 0-6-0T No. 16379 in LMS days.

'5' class 0-6-0T No. 9 sporting its G&SWR livery in Glasgow Museum of Transport.

Glasgow City Council (Museums)

The lessons of the rocking shafts drive to the valves when using Stephenson link motion were learned, for the class '45' 0-6-2T had its slide valves directly driven. Eighteen were built by North British in 1915 (4), 1916 (2) and 1917 (12) and put into use as intended. Their rugged construction followed closely that of the HR 0-6-4T and they had a substantial tractive effort of 22,080 lb. Such was their usefulness that in 1919 a further 10 were ordered by Peter's successor, Whitelegg, who cleared out any remaining Drummond paraphernalia and also had this batch fitted with right-hand drive. One of the latter batch actually made it into BR stock, the only G&SWR locomotive to achieve that goal. An indication as to the effect of wartime inflation on the railway's costs is to be found in the production costs of the 0-6-2Ts. In 1915/16 the six built were costed at £3,350 each. By 1917 when the next batch of 12 appeared this cost had risen to £4,560 apiece.

The final locomotive to carry the Drummond name was another tank, this time an 0-6-0T. It was for purely shunting purposes which had, up to then, been carried out by a few antiquated 0-4-0 tender locomotives. These had lasted because their short wheelbases were capable of travelling round some very sharply-curved track layouts found in some areas, notably in the Ardrossan and Greenock branches. To this end the centre driving wheels of this tank were flangeless. This design, given the class '5' designation, employed outside cylinders and Walschaert's valve gear and were devoid of all Drummond gadgets. Two of the three built in 1917 by North British survived until being withdrawn in 1934 and were sold to Llay Main Colliery in Denbighshire. This proved a happy move, for one lasted at the colliery until 1962 when it was withdrawn and stored long enough to be rescued for preservation. Taken back to Glasgow, it was restored and given a resting place in the Museum of Transport in that city. It remains there to this day, the only preserved example of Peter Drummond's design expertise.

One last project of Peter's was for a 4-6-0. Little has remained about the details of this, quite probably it was based on one of Dugald's designs and, as such, would have been a doubtful performer. The advent of World War I put an effective stop to any development of this design beyond the drawing board, and it faded into obscurity.

No further record of design studies has been found for the G&SWR days of Peter. For most of time on that railway Britain was approaching or involved in the war, so priorities were altered as the railways concentrated on keeping the network operating to maximum effect. New designs were put on one side as restrictions on the use of materials were introduced and the railways came under Government control. Industry needed supporting in its vastly increased output to meet the needs of the British forces on land, sea and in the air.

The pressure of work in wartime coupled with advancing years took its toll of Peter Drummond's health, for in 1918, despite carrying on in obviously failing health, on 30th March he left his office in considerable discomfort. He never returned to work, for after seeing his Doctor the diagnosis was not good, and after a three month painful battle with cancer of the bowel, he died on 30th June. Like his elder brother had been he was still in harness, not wishing to desert his post in a time of war. It seemed that the Drummond trait was not to encompass an honoured retirement. His eldest daughter, Jeanie was dispatched by her Doctor husband to be present to comfort her mother in her loss.

The two brothers had, between them, provided a wide range of locomotives for four Scottish and one English railways. Both had been responsible for some good and some indifferent performers and, it seems, were very stubborn about the need to minimise on gadgetry. Their management styles were abrasive, direct, and effective in that those who worked under them either toed the line or were soon disposed of. Dugald had by far the stronger personality, with Peter following his precepts when working under him, and having sundry advice and drawings put his way once he, too, had reached the position of Locomotive Superintendent.

Neither man would suffer fools gladly, but whilst Dugald's stubborn manner spilled over into his private life and contributed to his passing, Peter showed a dramatic change in character over the last three years of his life which may have contributed to the change in design philosophy at the end of his career. Whether an earlier transformation would have allowed his team to make their suggestions known is debatable, for one thing is certain, Dugald would definitely have made his feelings very clear.

Nevertheless, the two brothers made their mark on the British railway scene in the Victorian and Edwardian eras. They are a classic example of how to climb from humble beginnings to the top of a demanding profession, which in those days was quite rare. Their names were to live on in the various examples of their locomotives serving on the English and Scottish railways soon to be reorganized in the Grouping of 1923. What they would have thought of all that will never be known, doubtless some forthright statements would have ensued!

The Scottish traditions of solid engineering associated with both Drummonds lived on with Robert Urie at Eastleigh, now developing a range of new 4-6-0s, as well as improving many of Dugald's 4-4-0s and 0-6-0s, divesting them of many gadgets and ensuring for them a long and useful life, with many to enter BR service. The G&SWR lumbered on under Whitelegg until the Grouping of 1923 sucked it into the LMS empire and obscurity. Whilst many of Dugald's better designs lived on into Nationalisation days, Peter's engines, for both the HR and G&SWR, began to disappear throughout the 1930s during Stanier's huge restocking programme. Just the odd example lived on to see Nationalisation dawn before withdrawal and scrapping. At the time of writing, with but one example of a Drummond design in working order (the 'M7' on the Swanage Railway), their classic locomotives which graced the rails on both sides of the Border are but a memory to many. The brothers' lives, however, are recorded here in this biography to make their many achievements available to all who are interested in railway history.

Dugald Drummond Locomotives - Scottish Railways

Class	Type	First Batch	Subsequent Batches	No. Built	
North British Railway					
165	0-6-0T	1875	1876-8	25	
100	0-6-0	1876	1877	32	
474	2-2-2	1876	-	2	
476	4-4-0	1876	1878-9	12	
157	0-4-2T *	1877	-	6	
494	4-4-0T	1879	-	3	
34	0-6-0	1879	1880-3	101	
72	4-4-0T	1880	1881-4	30	
			Total	211	
Caledonian Railway					
294/711	0-6-0	1883	1884-97	244	
66	4-4-0	1884	1885-91	29	
13	4-4-0	1894	-	6	†
171	0-4-4T	1884	1886-91	24	
262	0-4-2ST	1884	-	2	
264	0-4-0ST	1885	1889-95	24	
123	4-2-2	1886	-	1	#
385	0-6-0ST	1887	1888-90	30	
80	4-4-0	1888	1891	12	
			Total	372	

* Later modified to 0-4-4T.
† Built by McIntosh in this year with minimal changes.
# The famous Caley 'Single', although often attributed to Drummond, was actually built by Neilson's for entry as an example of current practice at the Edinburgh International Exhibition of 1888. Many of the components were standard to the '66' class 4-4-0 and Dugald Drummond had clearly given his blessing to the project.

Dugald Drummond Locomotives - LSWR

Class	Type	First Batch	Subsequent Batches	No. Built	
-------	------	-------------	--------------------	-----------	
Locomotives					
M7	0-4-4T	1897	1898-1911	105	
700	0-6-0	1897	-	30	
T7	4-2-2-0	1897	-	1	
C8	4-4-0	1898	-	10	
T9	4-4-0	1899	1900-01	66	
F9	4-2-4T	1899	-	1	*
E10	4-2-2-0	1901	-	5	
K10	4-4-0	1901	1902	40	
L11	4-4-0	1903	1904-07	40	
S11	4-4-0	1903	-	10	
L12	4-4-0	1904	-	20	
F13	4-6-0	1905	-	5	
E14	4-6-0	1906	-	1	
G14	4-6-0	1908	-	5	
K14	0-4-0T	1908	-	5	
P14	4-6-0	1910	-	5	
T14	4-6-0	1911	-	10	
D15	4-4-0	1912	-	10	
			No. of locomotives	369	
Steam Railcars					
K11	0-2-2	1903	-	2	
H12	0-2-2	1904	-	2	
H13	0-2-2	1903	1904-06	13	
			No. of steam railcars	17	
Motor Train Engines					
C14	2-2-0T	1906	-	10	
S14	0-4-0T	1910	-	2	
			No. of motor train engines	12	
			Grand total	398	

* Known as 'Mr Drummond's Car' or 'The Bug'. Used for transporting Dugald around the LSWR on business and inspection tours.

Appendix Three

Peter Drummond Locomotives

Class	Type	First Batch	Subsequent Batches	No. Built
Highland Railway				
C	4-4-0	1898	1899-1906	20
K	0-6-0	1900	1902-07	12
A	4-6-0	1900	1902-17	19 *
V	0-6-0T	1903	1904	3
W	0-4-4T	1905	1906	4
U	4-4-0	1908	1909	6
X	0-6-4T	1909	1910-12	8
			Total	72
Glasgow & South Western Railway				
279	0-6-0	1913	-	15
131	4-4-0	1913	-	6
137	4-4-0	1915	-	6
16	2-6-0	1915	-	11
45	0-6-2T	1915	1916-17	18
1	0-6-2T	1919	-	10 †
5	0-6-0T	1917	-	3
			Total	69

* Further 50 built for the French State Railways.
† Built by Whitelegg to Peter Drummond's design.

Highland Railway 0-6-4T No. 15300 at Inverness in LMS days.

Appendix Four

Drummond Preserved Locomotives

Dugald Drummond

Class	Type	No.	Built		Location
			Year	By	

Caledonian Railway

123	4-2-2	123	1886	Neilson's	Glasgow Museum of Transport

London & South Western Railway

M7	0-4-4T	245	1897	Nine Elms	NRM
M7	0-4-4T	53	1905	Nine Elms	Swanage Railway
T9	4-4-0	120	1899	Nine Elms	NRM

Peter Drummond

Glasgow & South Western Railway

5	0-6-0T	9	1917	North British	Glasgow Museum of Transport

'M7' class 30053 arrives at Swanage 20th October, 2003. This particular locomotive used to be based at Bournemouth and work the branch before closure.   *Author*

Appendix Five

The Drummond 'Gadgets'

Much has been written about the Drummond 'gadgetry' applied to both Dugald's and Peter's designs. Dugald was a keen advocate of anything likely to improve the running costs by reducing fuel consumption in terms of coal burnt to evaporate a given quantity of water. This explains why he introduced feed-water heaters to raise the temperature of water fed to the boiler and thereby require less heat to turn it into steam. It is appropriate to discuss briefly the various innovations introduced by the brothers and give them a critical appraisal, for they have cropped up in many chapters of this biography and constitute an important feature of their approach to locomotive design and operation.

Despite the adverse comments made about much of the gadgetry introduced by the Drummonds, in theory many of them were logical features to enhance the performance and economy of their locomotives. The feed-water heating followed directly from Dugald's adherence to Stroudley principles, but added a further system to the locomotive requiring regular maintenance. Another disadvantage with this equipment was that the temperature rise of the feed water brought about the need to replace injectors with mechanical feed pumps which complicated matters somewhat. Injectors have no moving parts whereas pumps need to be duplicated to ensure that mechanical failure does not cause the engine to be failed.

Water tubes in the firebox were perfectly logical, this gave a substantial increase in heating surface at the point where the heat was at its maximum and, according to Dugald, assisted in the circulation of the boiler water around the firebox external surface. The increase in steaming was very evident but their location made firing difficult, particularly on long narrow grates, the 4-6-0s being a case in point. The best application of firebox heating surface enlargement was yet to come in the thermic syphon employed by Bulleid on his Pacifics in the 1940s. The further claim as their being an effective spark arrester was probably a reasonable one, but if they had been a really efficient spark arrester, the draughting would have suffered somewhat.

As far as easing the driver's task was concerned, the Drummond steam reverser was reliable and accurate, but rather inconveniently placed between the frames, making maintenance awkward.

On the '700' series 0-6-0, Dugald introduced his smokebox spark arrester. This arrangement necessitated a conical-shaped smokebox door, so the locomotives bearing this affair were easily identified whilst it was fitted.

Never an advocate of superheating as being developed on other railways, Dugald devised his own form of decidedly low-degree superheater, or 'steam-drier' as he preferred to call it. This apparatus was mounted in the smokebox and the resulting temperature rise was no more than 30-40 degrees, so any benefit it might have had was insignificant. Superheating at the time of the 4-6-0 development was beginning to be applied quite extensively now that the Schmidt and Robinson types were proven, but Dugald never did like using other's ideas and also had some misgivings on the effect of high temperature steam on the lubrication qualities of the available oils.

There was one further attempt in the superheating (Steam Drier) episodes. This was one of the 4-6-0s being given one extra superheating element in a flue tube of 3½ inches diameter which ran from the front tube plate to the firebox wrapper at the very top of the water space. It required a right angle bend to enable it to be connected at the top surface of the wrapper. This did not last long, for the obvious problem of the flue becoming exposed above the water level should this fall, thus resulting in overheating and fracturing. The experiment was soon terminated. One reference (Langridge) refers to 'T14' No. 458 being the particular locomotive involved.

This Adams class '135' has clearly been tinkered with by Dugald as witness the conical smokebox door. *John Scott-Morgan Collection*

Whilst some of the above features quickly disappeared, the smokebox spark arrester in its original form being a case in point, the majority of the remainder stayed so long as Dugald was in command. Much of the 'gadgetry', apart from the steam reversers, gradually began to be removed once Robert Urie had taken over, the rate of removal being slowed somewhat by the advent of World War I. Motive power, no matter how dubious, was urgently needed to deal with the increase in rail traffic in those years.

As for Peter's adherence to the features so vociferously promoted and incorporated by his brother, it is noticeable that whilst he did adopt some of Dugald's gadgets, he never applied them to all of his designs, particularly some of those to appear after the death of Dugald. He also adopted full superheating on the G&SWR, but by then his brother had died and was no longer around to wield any influence over him. The influence of Dugald's preferences had, indeed, been strong.

Appendix Six

Superheating Technology and Dugald Drummond

Having read some of the text of his talk to the LSWR Engineering Club in 1911, it is obvious that Dugald had a somewhat unusual view of locomotive drivers' capabilities when comparing them to their counterparts in shipping. He classed marine engineers as 'educated mechanics' who were capable of dealing with troublesome situations by their careful watch over the engines in their charge. As well they should, for the guidance of the vessel was in the hands of the Officers and crew on the bridge. By contrast locomotive drivers were, in his opinion, not sufficiently educated 'as to expect from them the same degree of intelligence'. Being a competent driver himself, it is not difficult to see the reasoning behind these remarks penned by him. He clearly realised the somewhat rigid adherence to driving techniques passed down by previous generations of drivers which, as locomotive technology moved forward, were made somewhat obsolete by that technology. Expansive driving - i.e. wide open regulator and short cut-off - was sometimes difficult to impress on his men. He also made the argument that the steam pipe being in the smokebox, some degree of dryness must be imparted to the saturated steam passing through. This is a debatable point. It depends surely on the speed of passage of the steam. This would restrict the 'drying' capacity available and may well have led to his arguments for a 'steam-drier' which, by offering a longer steam passage, may well impart a small degree of superheat. One wonders if this aspect played some part in his reluctance to implement high degree superheating and added to his other argument about adequate lubrication in high temperature conditions, and also of drivers not having the knowledge of how to deal with any such overheating problems that may occur. Hot boxes, yes, but cylinder lubrication was a different kettle of fish. The oils available during Victorian times were only satisfactory up to a certain temperature, certainly below that applicable to superheated steam, and the lubricating qualities of saturated steam were usefully employed to distribute this oil. Superheating dried steam and also presented the problem of reducing the lubrication of the cylinders, so calling for more oil of the type which could maintain its qualities at very high temperatures. An oil of that type was expensive and the age-old argument of 'is the increase in cost balanced by coal and water saving?' may well have raised its head. A bit presumptuous, one may think, particularly as other railways, notably the GWR, were introducing superheating with considerable success.

Another factor seemingly ignored by Dugald was that superheated steam had greater expansive properties than saturated steam, which was the root cause of much of the coal and water economy obtained from superheating. He, it seems, was reluctant or, more likely, unwilling to accept this simple fact. In this he had the backing of the encouraging results from his boiler pressure trials in 1889 on the Caledonian Railway. His design philosophy, driven by his Scottish sense of economy, was to keep everything as simple as possible, and thereby cost-effective. However, this simplicity trait appears to have been ignored when the four-cylinder 4-6-0s were being schemed. In passing it is worth noting that Urie was firmly of the opinion that four-cylinder locomotives were an expensive complication and would have pushed for two-cylinder designs if at all possible, as witness his immediate switch to such layouts once he had the CME's position. Another matter which influenced the Drummond approach to superheating was the Not Invented Here syndrome, a common fault with some CMEs. Those units which were prevalent in the early years of superheating practice were the Schmidt and Robinson types, the employment of which would have involved the payment of patent royalties, an unnecessary or unwanted cost, according to Dugald. He maintained that they were complicated and expensive to maintain in working order. Other CMEs overcame the royalty problem by designing their own version of the superheater, sometimes by a surprisingly simple design change which not only circumvented the payment but eased some of the problems of servicing inherent with the early versions.

In the background Robert Urie was quietly planning to bring about a proper superheating of locomotives, but cautiously held his cards close to his chest. This sort of stick-in-the-mud attitude by Dugald towards the end of his career seems to indicate that technical advances in thermal efficiencies were being dismissed as being beyond the scope of an ageing, very practical, engineer.

Where Dugald really scored was in the design features which gave his locomotives durability to withstand long and intensive use. He also paid attention to the front end and took the trouble to get his designers to aim for as smooth and short a steam passage as possible. A Drummond front end was usually a good one - particularly if it was two-cylindered, as witness the CR exercise to improve matters there.

Appendix Seven

The 'Double-Singles'

One of Dugald's arguments for the double-single was that it was possible to keep the traction force to a level more conducive to that which was less likely to produce slipping when starting or accelerating. Slipping caused extra wear on the locomotive, particularly the motion and tyres. In his eyes a single-driver was the best type to produce a free-running locomotive, he writes: 'It is the most economical and easiest running engine to work'. However, the single had disadvantages in starting due to its propensity to slip under heavy loads. Coupling the driving wheels to others of the same diameter produced extra adhesion, which latter would only have been possible on the single by increasing the driving axle load. There was also the fact that track loadings were restricted to specific values to ensure that rail damage did not occur, which limited high axle loadings.

If a locomotive had two independent sets of driving wheels, each set of wheels driven by its own pair of cylinders, i.e. a double-single, under ideal conditions the adhesion should be at a maximum at all times. This appears to be the reasoning behind the designing of the 4-2-2-0s and the persisting with that layout for a second batch to follow the prototype. To quote from page 63 of his Lectures to Enginemen book: 'If to work our heavy express trains at high speeds we are forced to use [two] large cylinders to obtain greater tractive force, we must do one of two things - either couple two or more pairs of wheels to obtain sufficient adhesion to prevent the wheels slipping, or use four cylinders of smaller diameter, and couple each pair of cylinders to separate wheels'. This, then is one basis of his reasoning for this design, however, immediately after this statement he goes on: 'To do this we require a larger boiler [which in fact was a major modification to the prototype in 1905] but we should have the advantage of being able to keep the weight for adhesion on each pair of wheels within reasonable bounds, and it would, in my opinion, solve the difficulty of securing greater tractive power with the minimum of dead weight'.

But then, the dynamics of an accelerating locomotive throws additional weight on the rear axle thereby reducing the weight on the front axles which, for a double-single of the Drummond layout, could well result in a slip on that axle. It was, after all, a Catch 22 situation.

The question of draughting also raises its head, in that should even a momentary slip on one pair of wheels occur, the exhaust beats would be out of phase, or uneven, from the ideal equally spaced and simultaneous pulses from two sets of cylinders. Draughting can be a sensitive issue for the steaming capacity of a boiler and maybe this partially goes to explain why the boiler was unable to provide sufficient steam on many occasions.

Suffice to say, these experimental express locomotives spent much time on shed being tinkered with and were never popular with all but a few crews, but had a surprising life of over 25 years before condemnation and scrapping.

This class 'E10' double-single has been coaled up for a future task and has some visitors on the footplate.   *John Scott-Morgan Collection*

Bibliography

A History of England by Keith Feiling, BCA.
A History of the Steam Locomotive by David Ross, Tempus.
A Pictorial Record of Southern Locomotives by J.H. Russell, OPC.
ARLE Minutes (notes on) - compiled by Geoffrey Hughes.
Beardmore - The History of a Scottish Giant by J.R. Hume and M.S. Moss, Heinemann.
British Locomotives of the 20th Century by O.S. Nock, BCA.
Caledonian Cavalcade by A.E. Glen, I.A. Glen with A.G. Dunbar, Ian Allan.
Dictionary of National Biography - Missing Persons by C.S.Nicholls (ed.), OUP.
Drummond Locomotives by Brian Haresnape, Ian Allan.
Experiments with Steam by Charles Fryer, Patrick Stephens Ltd.
Falkirk Library Services (for Polmont data).
General Register Office for Scotland - Archives.
Highland Railway Locomotives - Book 2 by J.R.H. Currie and J.L. Stevenson, RCTS.
Highland Council Genealogy Centre, Inverness Library.
History of the Southern Railway by C.F. Dendy Marshall, Ian Allan.
Institution of Civil Engineers, Proceedings.
Institution of Mechanical Engineers, Proceedings and Archives.
Lectures Delivered to Enginemen and Firemen of the L&SWR on the Management of Their Engines by D. Drummond, Waterlow & Sons, 1908.
Locomotive Adventure by H. Holcroft, Ian Allan.
Locomotives of the Glasgow & South Western Railway by David L. Smith, David & Charles.
Master Builders of Steam by H.A.V. Bulleid, Ian Allan.
Phoenix to the World by James Murray, Playright Publishing Pty Ltd.
Rail Centres: Brighton by B.K. Cooper, Ian Allan.
South Coast Railways - Brighton to Worthing by Vic Mitchell and Keith Smith, Middleton Press.
Southern Steam by O.S. Nock, David & Charles.
SR 150 by Patrick Whitehouse and David St John Thomas, David & Charles.
Steam from Waterloo by Col.H.C.B.Rogers, David & Charles.
Stroudley Locomotives by Brian Haresnape, Ian Allan.
The Aspinall Era by H.A.V. Bulleid, Ian Allan.
The Baillie for 1884 and 1914.
The Callander and Oban Railway by John Thomas, David & Charles.
The Drummond Greyhounds by D.L. Bradley, David & Charles.
The Four Great Railways by M. Bonavia, David & Charles.
The Highland Railway by H.A. Vallance, David & Charles.
The LSWR in the 20th Century by J.N. Faulkner, David & Charles.
The 'Scottish' 4-4-0 by Tom Middlemass, Pendragon Books.
The Skye Railway by John Thomas, David & Charles.
The South Western Railway by C. Hamilton Ellis, George Allen & Unwin.
The Southern King Arthur Family by O.S. Nock, David & Charles.
Their Work was Australian by Bobbie Hardy, Halstead Press, Sydney.
Twenty Locomotive Men by C. Hamilton Ellis, Ian Allan.
Under Ten CMEs by E.A. Langridge, Stephenson Locomotive Society Journal, 1973-5.

Index